# BUILDINGS
## AND
# LANDMARKS
## OF
# EDINBURGH

## Michael T.R.B. Turnbull

# Chambers

Published by W & R Chambers Ltd Edinburgh, 1989
Reprinted 1989

**British Library Cataloguing in Publication Data**
Turnbull, Michael, *1941-*
    Edinburgh buildings and landmarks.—
    (Chambers mini guides).
    1. Edinburgh. Buildings of historical
    importance
    I. Title
    941.3′4

    ISBN 0-550-20051-7

Cover design by John Marshall

Typeset by Bookworm Typesetting Ltd, Edinburgh
Printed in Singapore by
Singapore National Printers Ltd

# Contents

# Preface

This is a book about buildings. It is not so much about architecture as about events which took place in the buildings of Edinburgh and, where possible, about the *contents* of buildings today – those unique treasures of Edinburgh's past without which the present would be unintelligible.

A word of explanation: 'Edinburgh' has been defined for the purposes of the book by the present (1989) geographical boundaries of the City of Edinburgh District Council. Through the centuries 'Edinburgh' has meant many different things: the original cramped citadel expanded out of the Old Town into the New (1767) and then into the Northern New Town (1809). In 1856 Southside and Canongate reluctantly became part of Edinburgh; Portobello in 1896, Leith in 1920, along with Newhaven, Colinton, Cramond and Corstorphine. Finally, in 1975 came Queensferry, Balerno, Currie and Kirkliston.

*Note*
The precise location of Edinburgh's buildings and landmarks is clearly indicated in the text, which is arranged into convenient area locations. There is also a full index. However, readers and visitors to the city would be well advised to use this book in conjunction with a good map. This done, there should be little difficulty in locating the buildings and landmarks described.

Michael T.R.B. Turnbull

# SELECT READING LIST

*Edinburgh*, David Daiches, Hamish Hamilton, 1978
*Edinburgh (The Buildings of Scotland)* ed. Colin McWilliam, Penguin, 1984
*Edinburgh – The Story of a City*, E F Catford, Hutchinson, 1975
*Edinburgh Portraits*, Michael Turnbull, John Donald, 1987
*The Historic Houses of Edinburgh*, Wilmot Harrison (1893), repr. S R Publ., 1971
*In Praise of Edinburgh*, ed. Rosaline Masson, Constable, 1912
*Memorable Edinburgh Houses*, Joyce M Wallace, John Donald, 1987

I should like to acknowledge in particular the advice and help given to me by my colleague, the late Alasdair MacCallum, and the support I have received from the staff of the Edinburgh Room of the Central Library, George IV Bridge, Edinburgh.

To Mary

# OLD TOWN
## Edinburgh Castle

Power is the key to the Castle: its shape and position were deliberately chosen to protect and enhance political and military strength. Its plan, laboriously adjusted to meet changes in military technology, is as cunningly designed as the layers of an onion to protect a vulnerable heart. Bolted to a volcanic plug, levelled and terraced by military engineers, supported by subterranean vaults and screened by interlocking curtains of stone, the Castle dominates the landscape as far as the cold waters of the Firth of Forth, thundering with cannon, the muscular Lion of Scotland growling overhead.

By the Iron Age the Castle Rock was already a fortress: a basalt foundation 437 feet above sea-level, high above the woods and marshes below. By the sixth century it appears as the domain of King Mynydogg from which a party of armed horsemen rode to defeat at Catterick.

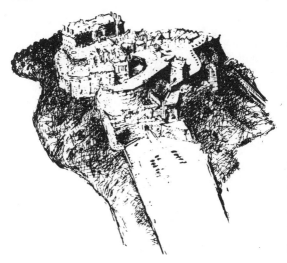

*Edinburgh Castle from the air – looking west.*

The earliest landscape of the Rock was buildings of stone and wood guarded by a wall of tree-trunks. To the west and the north the slopes were covered with grass. Access to the fort was by the 'Lang Stairs' (still visible today in its medieval form). All that remains of that ancient fortress, (the 'Maiden Castle' as it was called), is the narrow rectangular place of worship built around the year 1110 in the name of the saintly Queen Margaret of Scotland.

## The East Museum
*(off Crown Square)*

Devoted to uniform, equipment, weapons and paintings of The Royal Scots Greys, the Cavalry, the Navy, and the Royal Air Force in Scotland.

## The West Gallery
*(off Crown Square)*

Featuring the firearms and equipment, military drums, colours and uniforms of: the Royal Artillery, Scots Regiment of Guards, Scots Fusilier Guards, Royal North British Fusiliers, Scotch Brigade, King's Own Scottish Borderers, Royal Scots, Cameronians, Duke of Albany's Own Highlanders, Black Watch, Royal Highland Regiments, Seaforth Highlanders, Highland Light Infantry, Gordon Highlanders, 78th Highlanders, and the Argyll and Sutherland Highlanders. Two pikes, 11 and 18 feet long, are displayed. Commemorative medals, shooting awards, medals for bravery and devoted service, Regimental medals and Victoria and George Crosses are housed separately.

## Regimental Museums

The Royal Scots Regimental Museum is located below Foog's Gate while the Royal Scots Dragoon Guards Museum is off Hospital Square.

# The Story of the Scottish Soldier 1600-1914
*(North Hospital Block)*

The ground floor display consists of: A Soldier's Life in the 1790s, The Jacobites, Great Scots (1793-1816), The Battle of Waterloo. On the first floor are shown: Royalty in Uniform, A Scottish Appearance, Weekend Soldiers, The Crimean War, Home Service, The Yeomanry, and a room of prints and paintings showing The Martial Image.

# The Jacobite Room
*(east side of Crown Square: ground floor)*

Here are contained a number of relics of the Jacobite Risings and of the Battle of Culloden which finally put an end to them.

A jacket, trews, riding coat and glove said to have been Bonnie Prince Charlie's hang by the door, along with a shoe taken from his horse after Culloden and the stump of a thorn tree growing on the battlefield at Prestonpans.

Alongside the Burgess Ticket, presented on 3 January 1747 to William ('Butcher'), Duke of Cumberland when he was granted the Freedom of the City of Edinburgh, are the 'Culloden Pipes' (which belonged to a soldier from Argyll who served in the Jacobite army), a Highland target (shield) made of wood covered with cowhide and faced on the inside with deerskin, Highland dirks and broadswords, a Gaelic Bible and the Clan Colour of the Stewarts of Appin, which it is said 17 successive members died to preserve. It is torn by musket-balls and still stained with their blood. It was the only one of the Clan Colours to escape capture. The other twelve were burnt by the Common Hangman at the Cross of Edinburgh on 4 June 1746.

The song composed by Lady Caroline Nairne (1766-1845) is bitter-sweet in the light of the bloodshed at Culloden, the crushing severity of the

Hanoverian suppression and the Prince's ugly old age
and death in Rome in 1788:

> 'Royal Charlie's noo awa',
> Safely owre the friendly main;
> Mony a heart will break in twa,
> Should he ne'er come back again.
>
> Will ye no' come back again?
> Will ye no' come back again?
> Better lo'ed ye canna be,
> Will ye no' come back again?'

# The Royal Mile

## Castlehill

It is worth remembering that up to around 1550 most
houses were built with a timber frame filled in with
coloured plaster or clay; roofs were made of thatch or
covered with wooden tiles. Only after 1550 did stone
become the rule for houses and were roofs secured
with red clay pantiles. The reason for the change in
methods of construction was the ever-present danger
of fire, and as a result there are no wooden houses in
the Royal Mile today.

The best way to explore the Royal Mile is to start
from the **Castle Esplanade** and zig-zag across the street
from south to north (dipping at leisure into the wynds
and closes and the many museums which line the
route), down to Holyrood Palace.

Beginning on the Esplanade, where the Methodist
evangelist John Wesley (1703-91) often preached, we
come on the south side to **Cannonball House** which
takes its name from the two rusted cannonballs (one of
them fragmented) embedded in the west gable-end.
The house appears to date from 1630 when it was the
home of the merchant Alexander Mure.

Two theories exist as to why the cannonballs are
there. The first identifies them as having been shot
from the Castle's Half-Moon Battery in 1745 at the
time of the Jacobite occupation of Edinburgh and siege
of the Castle. However, it is unlikely that two
cannonballs would strike a wall in such exact
horizontal alignment. The second explanation is that

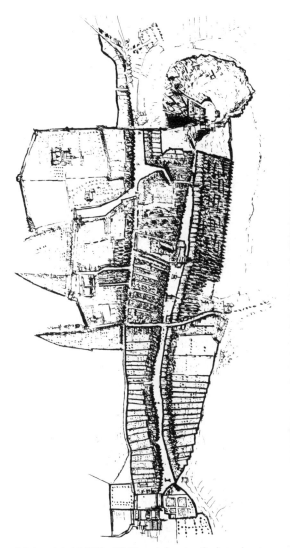

*Edinburgh in 1647 (the Old Town) showing the living herring-bone pattern of closes radiating from a central spine (the Royal Mile) with the Castle at its head and Holyrood as its tail.*

the cannonballs were markers inserted in 1681 by a German engineer, Peter Brusche, who was paid £3000 to lay a three-inch pipe from Comiston Springs Water House with its five springs – the Hare, the Fox, the Swan, the Lapwing and the Owl (*see*: the four remaining lead spring-mouths at Huntly House Museum). The cannonballs mark the water-level of the Comiston Springs.

On the north side is the **Castlehill Reservoir**, first constructed in 1681 (but replaced in 1851), with a capacity of almost two million gallons, supplied by the Swanston and Alnwickhill reservoirs and once feeding ten City wells.

Behind the Reservoir is **Ramsay Garden**, largely built in 1893 by Patrick Geddes (1854-1932) – the 'father of town-planning' – for his wife, around the octagonal central turret of the 'goose-pie' villa overlooking Princes Street Gardens. This was built in 1740 by the affable wig-maker and poet Allan Ramsay (1686-1758) as a love-nest and retirement haven (but used in 1745 by the Jacobite sharpshooters to take pot-shots at the Castle, which had refused to surrender). Below Ramsay Garden is the first of the 'Ragged Schools' opened in 1847 by the philanthropist and social reformer Dr Thomas Guthrie (1803-72) for the education and training of the many children 'at risk' from the effects of poverty or crime in the Edinburgh of his day.

Still on the north side we meet yet more of Patrick Geddes' work in the **Outlook Tower** (No 549 Castlehill), the lower part of which is 17th-century, built on the site of the mansion of the Laird o' Cockpen (the Ramsays of Dalhousie who gave their name to Ramsay Garden). The upper floors were added in 1853 when Maria Theresa Short installed her Camera Obscura to produce a panoramic view of the City.

In 1896 Geddes reorganised the interior into an outlook tower which began with a planetarium below the Camera, then the Scotland Room beneath, followed by surveys of Britain, Europe and the world, with two globes, one showing vegetation and the other geology. Geddes' aim was to awaken people to the need for conservation and the links between man and the environment. In 1945 a better lens and mirror system was installed and today displays of pinhole photography and holography are also included.

Crossing the road we find **Boswell's Court** (No 352), a 17th-century five-storey tenement named after the physician uncle of James Boswell (1740-95), Dr Samuel Johnson's pliable biographer. Dr Johnson dined there with Boswell in 1773.

The former Castlehill School (on the south side also) now houses a new **Scotch Whisky Heritage Centre** with exhibits demonstrating the distillation process and the history of Scotch Whisky production.

**Tolbooth St John's** church (built by James Gillespie Graham, 1842-44) was once the Victoria Hall for the Established Church General Assembly and contained a chair said to have belonged to John Knox. In the near future the church will house 'The Edinburgh Story', a day in the life of a family in 1594. In front of the church is a circle of cobblestones used as a traffic roundabout, but actually marking the site of the **Weigh House** or Butter Tron, where butter and cheese were weighed and sold. The first Weigh House was destroyed by the English in 1384. The 'Over Tron' was often the scene of public festivities. In 1554, for example, the Craftsmen's Church Play on Corpus Christi Day was performed here in front of Queen Mary of Guise (whose palace was across the road).

In 1614 the Town Council replaced the Tron with a new one but this building was used and demolished by Oliver Cromwell's troops in the siege of 1650. Finally in 1660 another Weigh House (whose cellar was used as a gaol) was erected; in 1745 it was taken over by the Jacobites as a guardhouse. In 1822 the Weigh House was demolished to widen the road for the visit of George IV to Edinburgh.

From the Weigh House to George IV Bridge the Royal Mile is also known as the 'Lawnmarket' (*Landmarket*), meaning that it was the designated selling area for traders not resident in the City.

## Lawnmarket

Where the **Assembly Hall** of the Church of Scotland now stands was once the Palace of Queen Mary of Guise (1515-60), widow of James (*see*: wooden panels in Queen Street Museum), Regent of Scotland (1554-60). She lived there after Holyrood had been burned down by the English under the Earl of Hertford in 1544. The New College and Assembly Hall (used with great effect as an apron-stage theatre during the Edinburgh Festival) were the work of William Playfair (1850) and David Bryce (1859) respectively and were constructed on the site of the Palace (demolished in 1861).

South of the Assembly Hall is the **Upper Bow**, once the head of a zig-zag road leading from the Grassmarket and used as an entry and exit by the Kings and Queens of Scotland and by criminals on their way to execution. James IV and James V passed this way, as did Mary Queen of Scots, Bothwell and Charles I. Down its cobbles Captain Porteous was dragged, and in the **West Bow** the wizard, Major Weir, committed his dark deeds. In 1834 the Upper Bow was separated from the West Bow by the construction of Victoria Street and Terrace.

Passing down into Victoria Street from Victoria Terrace it is worth making a detour to see the **Magdalen Chapel** (by arrangement with the Scottish Reformation Society at No 17 George IV Bridge). Founded by Michael Macqueen, a burgess, in the early years of the 16th century, it supported a chaplain and seven poor men whose function was to pray for the repose of the soul of Mary Queen of Scots, for the founder and his wife Janet and their descendants, and for the patrons of the Chapel (the Deacon and Masters of the craft of the Hammermen of the City of Edinburgh, whose responsibility the endowment was to be in future years). Attached to the Chapel was a Hospital.

By 1615 only the Chapel remained standing and this was adapted by the Hammermen to a Convening Hall. It was decorated in 1725 with the coats of arms of the eight trades in the Incorporation of Hammermen (Pewterers, Lorimers, Saddlers, Blacksmith, Cutlers, Locksmiths, Armourers and Shearsmiths). Four circular pieces of stained glass are almost the only Pre-Reformation windows still in existence in Scotland.

Climbing back to the north side of the High Street we find **Milne's Court** (No 513-523) built by the Royal

Master Mason Robert Mylne (1633-1710) in 1690, the seventh Mylne to be Master Mason to the House of Stewart. Mylne's son built Blackfriars Bridge over the River Thames and was a surveyor for the construction of St Paul's Cathedral. In 1745 some of the officers from Prince Charlie's Jacobite army lodged in Milne's Court. The west side was demolished in 1883, while the north and south blocks were restored and the east range rebuilt by Edinburgh University (1966-70), in 1971 gaining a Saltire Society Award for conservation.

Below the Assembly Hall is the wide expanse of **James Court** (Nos 507/501/493), with its three points of entry (west/mid/east) built by James Brownhill in 1727. The Court was the residence of well-off burgesses and had a garden planted with lime-trees. The philosopher David Hume (1711-76) lived on the third storey of the west stair from 1762 (a description of Hume in his library was given in Sir Walter Scott's *Guy Mannering* in the shape of Councillor Pleydell). While Hume was in France, from 1763 to 1766, Dr Hugh Blair (1718-1800), Professor of Rhetoric and Belles Lettres, lived in the house. Dr Blair's favourite reading was *The Arabian Nights* and *Don Quixote*. He was a very careful dresser, even placing a mirror flat on the floor and standing on tip-toe over it to look over his shoulder at the cut of his coat.

In 1773 James Boswell was tenant of the house when on 14 August he received Dr Johnson there.

It was while walking up the Lawnmarket to James Court, arm in arm with Boswell, that Dr Johnson made his famous remark about waste-disposal arrangements in the Old Town: 'It was a dusky night'; writes Boswell, 'I could not prevent his being assailed by the evening effluvia of Edinburgh.' Dr Johnson's comment was 'I smell you in the dark!'. In 1857 James Court was burned down and then later rebuilt.

## Gladstone's Land

The building known today as 'Gladstone's Land' dates in part from earlier than the 16th century. When Thomas Gledstanes and his wife bought it in 1617 the front of the stone and timber building was over 20 feet behind the present outer arches. This was the year of King James VI's joyful home-coming to Edinburgh, which signalled an expansion in self-confidence and commercial prosperity.

Gledstanes built out 23 feet from the house as he found it, doing away with the intimate wooden galleries on each floor. Other property owners were doing the same, so decreasing the width of the High Street with fashionable and solid stone fronts and arcades for shelter from the weather. Visitors to the building climbed the forestair on the pavement and then up the narrow turnpike. Often the forestair sheltered livestock, perhaps hens or a pig (although pigs were known to have been kept on the top floor of some buildings).

Edinburgh is sometimes credited with the invention of the 'sky-scraper' as the High Street houses often rose to six storeys on the street-front (as in Gladstone's Land) and as many as fifteen on the slope to the rear. Gladstone's Land (tenement) would have housed above the shop – the nobility on the first floor, the professionals (lawyers, doctors) on the second, the merchants on the third, the working-class on the fourth and the poor and destitute on the ramshackle top storey, frozen by the east wind. However, all walks of life met on the stairs, 'the democracy of the common stair'.

## Lady Stair's House

Lady Stair's House at No 477 Lawnmarket was completed in 1622 and re-created in 1895 for Lord Rosebery. Originally the house was in a cul-de-sac and had been the home of Elizabeth, Dowager Countess of Stair (d. 1759), a shining light in Edinburgh polite society in the early 18th century. Her first husband was Viscount Primrose, a man with a violent temper who treated her harshly.

One day she was in her bedroom when she caught a glimpse in a mirror of her husband creeping up behind her, a sword in his hand. Fearing for her life, she jumped out of the window into the street below. Soon after, Lord Primrose went abroad.

Some time later a fortune-teller came to town. Lady Primrose, disguised as a servant, went to him for news of her husband. The fortune-teller took her to a large mirror where she saw her husband walking up the aisle of a church with a young bride by his side. Suddenly she saw her brother approach and there was a duel and she saw no more. Months later her brother returned from abroad and confirmed the details of what she had seen in the fortune-teller's mirror. Robert Chambers tells this tale and Sir Walter Scott used it for one of his best short stories *My Aunt Margaret's Mirror*. There is a prophetic ring to the inscription above the door of Lady Stair's House: 'Feare the Lord and depart from Evil. 1622'.

In 1786 Robert Burns stayed on the first floor of the now demolished Baxter's Close (having arrived on 28 November), living in the lodging of John Richmond, a writer's clerk. From his window Burns could look out on Lady Stair's Close and it was here that Alex Nasmyth painted what has been called the most authentic likeness of the poet (*see*: Scottish National Portrait Gallery).

Crossing once more to the south we enter **Riddel's Court** (No 322) which contains Bailie Macmorran's House (a window-frame of which is in Huntly House). In 1593 Danish nobles banqueted with James VI and his Queen, Anne of Denmark, in the house of the unfortunate Bailie Macmorran, who was killed by the bullet of a rioting schoolboy at the High School in 1595. Here also David Hume lived before moving to James Court. The bust of Socrates was installed by Patrick Geddes.

Deacon Brodie, the respected craftsman and the hypocritical burglar, lived in the family home in **Brodie's Close** on the south side (his lantern and keys are in the possession of the Queen Street Museum). Today it is the home of the Roman Eagle Masonic Lodge. The now demolished Buchanan's Court, the birthplace of David Hume, the philosopher, was next-door.

11

# National Library of Scotland

A short diversion south along George IV Bridge brings us to the National Library of Scotland, the main Scottish reference library, and as a library of legal deposit, entitled to claim a copy of all printed works published in the United Kingdom and in the Republic of Ireland.

The National Library in 1925 became the successor to the Advocates Library, which was founded in 1680 by Sir George Mackenzie (1636-91); among the Keepers of the Advocates Library was the philosopher David Hume. The earliest book in the National Library is a copy of the Gutenberg Bible of 1455. The earliest books printed in Scotland (eleven verse pamphlets printed in Edinburgh by Chepman and Myllar in 1508) are also in the Library, forming part of a collection of almost 700 works dating from the 15th and 16th centuries.

Among other books published by Chepman is a copy of the Aberdeen Breviary (Edinburgh 1510), the only large work by Chepman which survives, and another copy of the first volume of the Breviary brought to Edinburgh from Leningrad in Russia at the time of the Revolution. Among the Library's special collections are those on bakery and confectionery, phrenology, shorthand, accounting and printing; the Walter B Blaikie Collection is entirely devoted to Jacobite material. Among the extensive collections of maps are those of Edinburgh engravers and publishers such as the Lizars and the Bartholomews.

# The Central Library

The Edinburgh Room of the Central Library contains the most extensive range in the world of printed information on the City of Edinburgh (over 68 000 items). The material at the disposal of the general public includes colour transparencies (over 6000), black and white lantern slides, maps and plans, newspapers (from the mid 18th century), over 300 periodicals, over 11 000 photographs and prints, an extensive collection of press-cuttings (indexed), rare and valuable materials, and valuation and voters rolls. Although generally speaking the work of authors born in Edinburgh is available (for reference) in the Edinburgh Room, the works of authors (such as Robert Louis Stevenson or Sir Walter Scott) who are considered to be of national importance are held in the Scottish Library on the floor below.

## High Street

From George IV Bridge to the Netherbow Port the Royal Mile is known as the 'High Street'. In Edinburgh's case this is doubly appropriate as not only are the buildings all several storeys high but the roadway itself is high above sea-level.

In **Libberton's Wynd** (now demolished), which once ran near the line of George IV Bridge, on the south side of the High Street, the 'Man of Feeling', Henry Mackenzie, was born in 1745. It was also the site of the famous John Dowie's tavern, the biggest room of which held fourteen persons and the smallest ('The Coffin') six at a pinch. David Hume frequented the tavern, Robert Burns found consolation in 'The Coffin' in 1786 (as his admired predecessor Robert Fergusson had) and so did the portrait-painter Sir Henry Raeburn. The beer served was Archibald Younger's ale, 'a potent fluid, which almost glued the lips of the drinker together, and of which few, therefore, could dispatch more than a bottle' (so wrote Robert Chambers). Speciality of the house was Nor' Loch trout (haddock stuffed and fried in breadcrumbs).

Three brass plates mark the site of public executions: here William Burke was put to death for his part in 'body-snatching', and the last public hanging (that of the murderer George Bryce) took place here in 1864, after the demolition of the Tolbooth in 1817 (at whose west end executions were carried out on the flat roof of a two-storey end building).

A brief diversion north from the High Street leads to **Bank Street** and the headquarters of the Bank of

Scotland, the original 1806 structure rebuilt in 1863 by David Bryce (with additions such as a 'Cyclops Eye' window).

Returning to the High Street the first building on the north side is the Sheriff Court (built in 1937) where a very wide variety of criminal and civil cases are dealt with; previously the Court had been in George IV Bridge.

To the south is the legal heart of Scotland: **Parliament Square** (which occupies the area east, south and west of St Giles), Parliament House with the supreme criminal court in Scotland (the High Court of Justiciary), the Supreme Civil Court (the Court of Session), the Signet and Advocates Libraries. To the west stands the headquarters of Lothian Regional Council. In previous times Parliament Square was a warren of rickety booths and workshops precariously attached to the walls of St Giles and around the Parliament House. Although this haphazard collection of booths was an undignified presence in the shadow of St Giles, the Town Council allowed only the finer crafts to trade there. Parliament Close therefore was monopolised by booksellers, watch-makers and goldsmiths (such as George Heriot) as well as coffee shops, where much legal business was transacted.

The most famous coffee shop was that of Peter Williamson (1730-99), 'Indian Peter' as he was called, from his having been kidnapped at the age of eight in his home town of Aberdeen and sold as a slave in Philadelphia. During his days in America he was captured and scalped by Red Indians, and taken prisoner by the French. Williamson eventually obtained his freedom, became a planter and came to Edinburgh where he opened a coffee house and tavern. Williamson was also a printer, publisher and bookseller; he started the first penny post in Edinburgh and produced the first Edinburgh street directory.

One important landmark no longer exists: the **Luckenbooths** (lockable shops) which ran in the middle of the High Street north of St Giles forming the 'Stinking Stile', a narrow defile thick with mud and

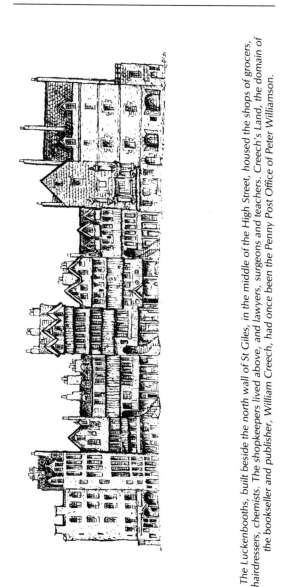

*The Luckenbooths, built beside the north wall of St Giles, in the middle of the High Street, housed the shops of grocers, hairdressers, chemists. The shopkeepers lived above, and lawyers, surgeons and teachers. Creech's Land, the domain of the bookseller and publisher, William Creech, had once been the Penny Post Office of Peter Williamson.*

slops along the side of the Kirk. Although the Luckenbooths were mainly permanent shops, the west end of the long, tall and thin cluster of buildings was formed by the Old Tolbooth, built in about 1386 and used variously as a meeting-place for the Scottish Parliament, for the Town Council, as a tax collection office and, most memorably, as the town gaol till its momentous demolition in 1817. The Luckenbooths dated from about 1460 and consisted of seven timber tenements between four and six storeys high. In 1728 Allan Ramsay opened the first circulating library in Britain on the first floor of the east end of the Luckenbooths, and 58 years later William Creech, publisher and bookseller, set up his premises immediately below.

The **Krames** (probably from a Dutch word) first appeared in 1550. Lord Cockburn remembers that 'their little stands, each enclosed in a tiny room of its own, and during the day all open to the little footpath that ran between the two rows of them, and all glittering with attractions, contained everything fascinating to childhood, but chiefly toys. It was like one of the Arabian Nights' bazaars in Bagdad. The Krames was the paradise of childhood.'

## St Giles High Kirk

St Giles is the parish church of Edinburgh, built soon after the town received the status of a 'burgh' in 1130. Although the 12th-century north doorway with its Romanesque decoration survived till the 1790s, there is now virtually no trace of the original building except one scallop capital and a recently-discovered corbel carved into the face of an animal. In 1385 St Giles and the rest of Edinburgh were burned by the English army. Recent archaeological investigation has found a large quantity of fragments of cooking-pots, jugs and storage vessels (all of white pottery from the 12th and 13th centuries, produced on a potter's wheel).

Where Parliament House now stands was the site of the manse and garden of the parish priest of St Giles (which in later years also contained the public school of Edinburgh. Most of the land stretching from the south side of St Giles to the Cowgate was taken up with the town cemetery.

A number of oak coffins were found in 1844 some 14 feet below ground-level under the south part of Parliament House. In 1867 Lord Provost William Chambers suggested the restoration of the church: in the course of this work (mainly funded by Chambers) several tons of human bones were moved from the ground under the church and reverently re-interred in Greyfriars burial-ground. During the construction of the Thistle Chapel in 1910 more burials were found four feet below Parliament Square: this explains the rather bizarre position of what is believed to be the grave of John Knox (parking space No 44, below the statue of Charles II).

In 1981-82 archaeologists found 114 human skeletons and from the many pins that were also discovered it appears that most people were buried in shrouds fastened by metal pins and that only the wealthier and more important members of the community were buried inside the church. An interesting feature of the burials is that almost everyone in those times had good teeth since they lived before the introduction of cane sugar!

After the church was damaged by Richard II in 1385 rebuilding began with five new chapels to the south and more construction to the north and east. A relic of St Giles (his arm-bone) was an important donation to the church at this time.

St Giles Kirk was raised to 'collegiate' status in 1466. This meant that the staff of the church would now have a religious community with a Provost at its head, a sacristan under him, fourteen canons (priests), and a choir-master with four choristers: the importance of music in worship is apparent. Gavin Douglas (1474-1522), son of the Earl of Angus, became Provost in 1503. His ecclesiastical achievements are largely forgotten, but his muscular, ringing poetry lives on in lines such as his description of a wet winter evening in Edinburgh in 1512:

'Mountain-tops sleekit with their snaw ower-heilds
On ragged rockes of hard harsk whin-stane;

17

Sharp sops of sleet and of the snipand snaw.
The plain streetes and every high way
Was full of flushes, dubbes, mire and clay.'

Douglas was perhaps responsible for the religious society who commissioned the Fetternear Banner of 1540 (*see*: Queen Street Museum), that is, the Confraternity of the Holy Blood of St Giles Collegiate Kirk, among whose members was James IV. The banner shows the importance of religion to the lay community of the burgh.

The church contained many fittings to make attendance more comfortable and instructive: a clock, a brazier, an organ, a lectern and a pulpit. At the time of the Reformation (1560), the relic of St Giles was handed over to the Dean of Guild. The wooden statue of the saint was carried in procession to the Nor' Loch and unceremoniously dumped into the water (no doubt suitably weighted), and the church gold and silver vessels were sold and the proceeds used for the benefit of the town. The medieval screens and furnishings were destroyed.

The 44 altars in the church were removed and the compartments (each privately owned) taken away to make one communal church. This created more room than the congregation needed and so the Town Council used part of the west end as a new Tolbooth and the east end as a school. In the central tower storks once built their nests close to the Great Bell (cast in Flanders and erected in 1460). For four months in 1571 the steeple of St Giles was held by troops loyal to Mary Queen of Scots and fortified. By 1572 John Knox (the minister of St Giles) was 'so weak that he had to be lifted into the pulpit by two servants'. The church accordingly was sub-divided again and in 1578 three separate congregations worshipped in it.

When in 1633 Charles I made St Giles into a Cathedral under the hated English episcopal system, much renovation took place and the church once again lost its sub-divisions. Popular resistance came to a head in 1637 when the vegetable seller, Jenny Geddes, picked up a folding-stool during a service and threw it at the Dean as he stood in the pulpit. The sub-divisions of the church returned, however, in

1639 and were in existence in various combinations until finally removed in 1882 under a scheme initiated by Lord Provost William Chambers.

Often observed but seldom noticed, the stained glass windows of St Giles seldom get the attention they deserve. There are some 14 memorial windows and about 19 others. Entering the church by the north door, turn left: the first window was erected in memory of William and Robert Chambers by Ballantine of Edinburgh, and represents the rebuilding and dedication of the Temple at Jerusalem (like the second window, in memory of William Chambers' work for St Giles).

The clerestory windows high overhead commemorate the Craftsmen of Edinburgh (such as the Wrights, the Masons, the Goldsmiths and Barber-Surgeons). The Montrose window (in the Chepman Aisle) lists the fellow-soldiers of Montrose and the clans which supported him. In the Moray Chapel we can see depicted the Assassination of the Earl of Moray, and John Knox preaching at his funeral service. In the Argyll window (St Eloi's Chapel) the Arms of the leaders of the Covenanters are shown. Of greatest artistic interest is the window in the west gable (north side) by William Morris and designed by Burne-Jones. Finally the central west window (dedicated in 1985) is a tribute to Robert Burns and represents the Natural World, the Brotherhood of Man and the Supremacy of Love. The window is the work of an Icelandic artist trained at Edinburgh College of Art, Leifur Breidfjord.

## Parliament Hall

The hammerbeam roof of the Hall is made of Danish oak installed in 1639 to provide room for the Scottish Parliament to meet. From 1707 when the Scottish Parliament was dissolved, the Hall has been given over to the needs of the Scottish Law Courts whose Outer and Inner Houses and High Court are contained in the remainder of Parliament House.

On the west side of Parliament Hall are paintings of Sir Thomas Hope, King's Advocate (1626-39) by George Jamesone, partnered by Archbishop Spottiswood, Lord High Chancellor (1635-39) and Archibald, 1st Lord Napier, the eldest son of the inventor of logarithms, John Napier. James Dalrymple, Viscount Stair (1619-95), author of the standard *Discourse upon the Laws and Customs of Scotland in Matters Criminal*, stands beside Lord President Duncan Forbes (1685-1747), who single-handedly administered Scotland during the repressive subjugation of Scotland following the Battle of Culloden in 1745 and moderated the retribution of the Hanoverians. On the east wall Archibald, Earl of Ilay (afterwards the 3rd Duke of Argyll) surveys the parading advocates and their clients in a painting by William Aikman. The Earl was Lord Justice General (1710) and Lord Justice Clerk in 1714.

The Great South Window installed in 1868 shows the inauguration of the Court of Session and College of Justice by James V on 27 May 1532. The window was designed and made at the Royal Bavarian Glass Factory in Munich, one of Edinburgh's twin cities.

Visiting Parliament Hall in 1867 Thomas Carlyle gives the following description of the scene: 'An immense Hall, dimly lighted from the top of the walls, and perhaps with candles burning in it here and there; all in strange *chiaroscuro*, and filled with what I thought a thousand or two of human creatures; all astir in a boundless buzz of talk, and simmering about in every direction, some solitary, some in groups.

By degrees I noticed that some were in wig and black gown, some not, but in common clothes, all well-dressed; that here and there on the sides of the Hall, were little thrones with enclosures, and steps leading up; red-velvet figures sitting in said thrones, and the black-gowned eagerly speaking to them – Advocates pleading to Judges.'

In the Advocates Library it is worth asking permission to view the standard of the Earl Marshall of Scotland carried at the Battle of Flodden in 1513 by the standard-bearer 'Black' John Skirving of

Plewland Hill. He was taken prisoner at the battle having previously hidden the banner under his clothing. The banner bears the arms and motto of the Family of Keith: 'Veritas Vincit' (Truth Conquers).

## The Signet Library

In the vestibule are busts and portraits of distinguished solicitors, including Sir Walter Scott WS (also the son of a solicitor) wearing a plaid. At the top of the imperial stair is Sir John Watson Gordon's portrait of Sir Charles Hope (Lord President and Lord Justice General (1811-41) standing in Parliament Square. On the right side of the stairs is David Boyle, Lord Justice General (1840-52), also by Gordon, while the landing outside the Upper Library has a portrait of Robert Blair, Lord President (1808-11) by Sir Henry Raeburn, and other paintings of George Drummond and Sir George Chalmers.

## The Mercat Cross

The **Mercat Cross** was a designated place of public sale and purchase for the merchants of Edinburgh. It consisted of a wide octagonal base (with steps for sitting on or resting containers), a platform above (for public proclamations, fitted with spouts for drainage or pouring wine out on festive occasions) and, at the top of a tall stone shaft, a heraldic device and a cross (intended to bring home the need for fairness and sincerity in business transactions). In addition, the Mercat Cross was a recognisable place to meet and, inevitably, the haunt of gossips and cadies.

Opposite **Fishmarket Close** (on the south side) a large circle of cobbles marks the former location of the Mercat Cross, first erected in the 12th century in the middle of the High Street in a line between the present Cross and the City Chambers. This medieval

*The Mercat Cross.*

Cross was taken down in 1617 and moved east to the head of Fleshmarket Close. In 1756 the Cross was demolished to widen the road for traffic (the new Royal Exchange had made it redundant) and it was not until 1885 that the Cross was re-erected by William Gladstone, some yards to the west, where it now stands in Parliament Square.

At the Mercat Cross state proclamations were made regarding the death and succession of monarchs, and it is said that on the night before the Scottish defeat at Flodden in 1513 ghostly heralds were seen proclaiming the list of the ten thousand names of those who were to die in the battle. At the Cross state criminals were executed (Montrose, Huntly, the Argylls and Warriston), and the banners of the Highland clans defeated at Culloden were burnt by the public executioner.

Walking down through **Byers' Close** (No 373) on the north side we are aware of the tall, ship-like form of the mansion of Adam Bothwell (c 1530-93), Bishop of Orkney and Commendator of Holyrood. Bothwell, a career minister with an instinct for survival, married Mary Queen of Scots to the Earl of Bothwell in May 1567 and later (as a Protestant) crowned James VI at Stirling two months afterwards.

Sir William Dick (1580-1655), a wealthy merchant trading from the Baltic to the Mediterranean (and Provost of Edinburgh in 1638), was a later tenant. According to Robert Chambers, Oliver Cromwell was in the habit of sitting in the north window-bay of an adjacent house to watch his navy on manoeuvres in the Forth. When the building was restored in 1977 six earthenware pots were found set into the wall; these are thought to be 'acoustic jars' positioned so as to improve the acoustics of the house for private concerts.

The names of houses in the Old Town changed over the years as different occupiers came and went, so one house could have many names from generation to generation. **Advocate's Close** (No 357) is named after one particular advocate: Sir James Stewart (1635-1713), Lord Advocate. It was also the home of Andrew Crosbie (the model for Sir Walter Scott's Councillor Pleydell in *Guy Mannering*) and Sir John Scougall, a Court painter during the reign of William and Mary. **Warriston Close** (No 323) was John Knox's manse (1560-66). Later Archibald Johnston of Warriston (Lord Warriston, the judge) lived there (1611-63). He was one of the leaders of the Covenanters, a principal framer of the National Covenant and was executed for his beliefs.

## City Chambers

The former **Royal Exchange** was built to give a more leisurely covered area for City merchants to do their business in, after the unsavoury but exciting scrabble of wheeling and dealing at the Mercat Cross. It is the only 18th-century building in the High Street and in its heyday was provided with shops, coffee houses – where real negotiation could take place, and a Customs House. Today the building functions as a seat of local government (the City of Edinburgh District Council).

## Mary King's Close

Before leaving the City Chambers, a visit to Mary King's Close, sunk deep below the back of the buildings, is recommended. The Royal Exchange was built over the top of the cobbled surface of the old close, which had been unoccupied for many years as it was thought that the shops and houses were haunted by those who had died from the Plague in the 17th century. In the late 18th century a Mrs Coltheart was sitting in her house in Mary King's Close reading her Bible when she looked up and saw a ghostly head floating in the room. Although her husband did not believe her he eventually saw the head also, as well as a child and an arm. The room filled with ghastly figures, then suddenly there was a hollow groaning and everything vanished. Today (by arrangement with the City Chambers) it is possible to join a guided party to the Close and see exactly what Edinburgh's High Street was like in those far-off days.

A plaque on the City Chambers recalls that the house of Sir Simon Preston of Craigmillar (Provost in 1566-67) was once on that site. In his house Mary Queen of Scots spent her last night in Edinburgh on 15 June 1567 after her defeat at Carberry. On the following evening she was removed to Holyrood and then taken to Loch Leven Castle.

Crossing the High Street to the south side we find **Old Fishmarket Close** (No 190) which was ravaged by two great fires in 1700 and 1824. The old buildings (which had risen to 15 storeys at the back) were destroyed as far down as the Tron, and replaced with houses of much reduced proportions.

In **Craig's Close** (No 265 on the north) were the premises of Andrew Hart who brought out an edition of the Bible in 1610. Other publishers and printers lived there in later years: Provost William Creech, Archibald Constable and William Smellie, whose premises were visited by Burns and by Scott. Craig's Close also housed Currie's Tavern whose speciality was 'pap-in', made with beer and whisky curried with oatmeal, and 'het-pint' made from mulled wine topped with whipped white of egg.

**Old Post Office Close**, as its name implies, was the site of the first Post Office in Edinburgh, in the reign of George I (1660-1727). At that time only one man delivered letters for the whole of Edinburgh (the Old Town).

**Anchor Close** (No 241 north) was the printing-house of William Smellie (1740-95) where he printed the first edition of the Encyclopaedia Britannica (1781) and with William Creech brought out the second 1787 (Edinburgh) edition of Burns' poems.

Also in the Close was the notorious Anchor Tavern owned by Dawnay Douglas. The visitor, according to Robert Chambers, 'found himself in a pretty large kitchen – a dark, fiery Pandemonium, through which numerous ineffable ministers of flame were continually flying about.' Dawnay's wife could be seen in her enormous head-dress, her gown decorated with daisies the size of sunflowers and tulips as big as cabbages. Here was the meeting-place of the 'Crochallan Fencibles', a mock-military organisation named after a Gaelic song that was the proprietor's favourite. William Smellie, the founder of the club, introduced Robert Burns to the membership after editing sessions at his publishing house. In the Close the parents of Sir Walter Scott lived till 1771.

Moving eastwards the next close is **Geddes Entry** (No 233 north). Here was the meeting-place of the Cape Club (*see*: Huntly House Museum – Edinburgh Social Clubs – Room 11).

**North Foulis Close** (No 299 north) housed two of Edinburgh's greatest characters: on the ground floor was the shop of James Gillespie (1725-97), snuff-grinder and philanthropist (*see*: Huntly House – basement); on the first floor lived (and died) the inimitable barber and caricaturist John Kay (1742-1826) whose wickedly perceptive etchings of Edinburgh folk were published in his *Edinburgh Portraits*.

Immediately to the east is **Old Stamp Office Close** (No 221). Here was once Fortune's Tavern where the Lord High Commissioner of 1754 held levées and from where he walked in state to St Giles (and which was also the meeting-place of the Poker Club, which supported the setting up of a militia for Scotland). The New or Royal Bank had its offices in the Close from its institution in 1727 until 1753.

It was to a finishing-school in the Close that Flora MacDonald (1722-90) came in 1740, a skilful player on the spinet and a delightful singer of Gaelic songs, to live in the care of her guardian, the beautiful Susanna, Countess of Eglinton, second wife of the 9th Earl, who lived with her seven elegant daughters. To Susanna the poet Allan Ramsay dedicated his first book of songs. It was one of the sights of Edinburgh to see the Eglinton ladies set out in the evenings for the Old Assembly Rooms across the road, each in her gilded sedan chair.

On the south side (below **Old Assembly Close**) is **New Assembly Close** (No 142) with its New Assemblies Hall of 1766. Here the passion for dancing assemblies was only partly satisfied as the ardour of the young and handsome was dampened by the rod of iron with which the mistresses of the assemblies regulated the dancing.

When the Assembly Rooms in George Street opened in 1786 the smaller High Street premises were gradually abandoned. In 1780 the King's Arms Tavern had opened in the Close and later the Lodge St David met there (which Sir Walter Scott attended). From 1814-47 the Commercial Bank took over the site; from 1884 it was a children's shelter until 1974 when the **Edinburgh Wax Museum** arrived.

The Wax Museum's slogan is 'Scotland's History

Brought to Life'. Inevitably many of the displays are of events that took place in Scotland's capital and of people who lived there. The events include the arrival of Mary Queen of Scots at Leith, the murders of Rizzio and Darnley, and the execution of Mary; the people include Sir Walter Scott, Sir Henry Raeburn, Lord Cockburn and Adam Smith, Robert Louis Stevenson, John Knox, the Marquis of Montrose, Sir Arthur Conan Doyle, Sir Harry Lauder and Sean Connery. The Chamber of Horrors includes Deacon Brodie, Burke and Hare and Major Weir the Wizard.

Crossing north to **Fleshmarket Close** (No 199) we are at the site of the Meat Market. In a cellar at the foot of the stair William Creech the printer and publisher of Burns started in business, while in Cameron's Tavern the Marrow-bone Club met. On the west side of the third floor lived Henry Dundas (1742-1811), 'the uncrowned king of Scotland'.

On the south side of the Royal Mile the tall grey steeple of the **Tron Kirk** points to the sky, a building plaintively seeking a new lease of life. Built in 1636-47 by John Mylne (1611-67) to accommodate the Presbyterians ousted from St Giles when it became an episcopalian Cathedral under Charles I, the Tron was so named after the public weighing-beam used to measure salt. It was constructed over the original Marlin's Wynd (said to include the grave of Merlioun, the French causeway expert). In the great fire of 1824 the Tron steeple was burnt and had to be demolished. Today the foundations of the Tron have been excavated to reveal the early shape of the High Street and the method of street-paving adopted by the early road engineers.

## St Cecilia's Hall

An interesting diversion can be made south down Niddry Street to **St Cecilia's Hall**, which has its origin in the St Cecilia's day concert of 1695 when 19 amateur gentlemen musicians and eleven professional teachers of music met to play together. Many private concerts followed over the next ten years, but it was not till 1728 that the Musical Society of Edinburgh was finally inaugurated at its regular meeting-place, Patrick Steil's tavern, 'The Cross Keys', near Parliament Close. In 1763 St Cecilia's Hall was completed (designed by the energetic Robert Mylne). In the foyer is a copy of the minutes of a meeting of the Directors of the Edinburgh Musical Society on 19 July 1759 when George Drummond, Lord Provost, was Deputy Governor.

St Cecilia's Concert Hall is the oldest concert hall in Scotland and is said to have been based on the opera house of Parma. A contemporary description of 1779 comments: 'It is oval in form, the ceiling a concave elliptical dome, lighted solely from the top by a lanthorn. Its construction is excellently adapted for music; and the seats ranged in the room in the form of an amphitheatre are capable of containing a company of about five hundred persons.'

Below the Tron Kirk the High Street is crossed by the 'Bridges': **North Bridge** (built in 1769 and widened in 1896) and **South Bridge** (opened in 1788). **Niddrie Wynd** (now Niddry Street) once ran south to the Cowgate at the foot of which was St Mary's Chapel, the oldest authenticated Freemasons Lodge in the world, demolished in 1788.

On the line of the North Bridge was **Cap and Feather Close** (now demolished) where the poet Robert Fergusson was born. Three elegant marble plaques from the house of Allan Ramsay (which stood a little further east) can be seen in the Royal Bank of Scotland (North Bridge Branch) set into the interior south wall, the top of an ornamental fireplace with swags and thistles.

Ramsay (a burgess in 1710) opened a wig shop in the Grassmarket two years later and at the same time helped to found the Jacobite Easy Club in the same year. By 1724 he was in his High Street publishing house ('at the sign of the Mercury') and from here he issued *The Ever Green* (filled with medieval Scottish poetry) and his play *The Gentle Shepherd* in 1725 when he moved to the first floor of the Luckenbooth beside St Giles. There he started the first lending library in Britain.

**Carrubber's Close** (No 135 north) was in 1450 the

home of the merchant William Carriberis and was the home of Archbishop Spottiswood (1565-1639) of St Andrews, Lord Chancellor of Scotland who in 1633 crowned Charles I at Holyrood. From 1688 the Close became a refuge for Jacobite sympathisers. When the Episcopalians were expelled from St Giles in 1689, Alexander Rose, Bishop of Edinburgh, founded Old St Paul's at the bottom of the Close (at first the congregation had worshipped in a wool store).

The Seabury Chapel commemorates Bishop Samuel Seabury, the first Bishop of the American Episcopal Church, who worshipped there as a student of medicine at Edinburgh University and who was consecrated Bishop in Scotland in 1784. Among the other members of the congregation were Baroness Nairne the song-writer, William Aytoun the poet, and Sir Henry Raeburn, Scotland's greatest portrait painter.

Allan Ramsay was a secret Jacobite sympathiser and in November 1736 he opened a theatre in Carrubber's Close; however, this was shut down in 1737 by the magistrates under the Licensing Act and the building reopened as the Whitfield Chapel. This in turn became 'the Celebrated Cathedral of the Prince of Darkness' when occupied by an atheist club in 1858, but by May of that year it had been consecrated as The Carrubber's Close Mission where Sir James Young Simpson was in 1865 running a medical dispensary. The Whitfield Chapel was demolished in 1872 and the foundation stone of the present Mission was laid in 1883.

**Bishop's Close** (No 129 north) was built by Thomas Sydeserf (1581-1663), Bishop of Brechin, then of Galloway and finally of Orkney. This was the birthplace of Henry Dundas (later Lord Melville) in 1742. In the Close lived Louis Cauvin, founder of the Cauvin Hospital for Boys at Duddingston (his portrait is in the Dean Education Centre, Belford Road — formerly the Dean Orphanage). In the winter of 1786-87 Cauvin gave Robert Burns three French lessons a week in the Close.

On the south side another brief diversion is called for down **Blackfriars Street**, named after a monastery founded in 1230 by Alexander II. This was also the scene of the bloody street-fight in 1520 known as

'Cleanse the Causeway' between the Douglases and the Hamiltons. At the foot of the street was the palace of Cardinal Beaton (1494-1546) who was involved in the battle. Near his palace Walter Chepman and Andrew Myllar set up their press and printed the first book in Scotland in 1506.

**Bailie Fyfe's Close** (No 107 north) was a Senior Bailie's house in 1686. When he was eight, Francis Jeffrey (1773-1850), the advocate and founder of *The Edinburgh Review*, went to school hère; Nathaniel Gow (1766-1831), son of Neil Gow, taught violin and piano in the Close (he sometimes played for George IV's private functions in London).

'Heave Awa House' in **Paisley's Close** (No 101 north) was the site of a dramatic accident in 1861 when a tenement collapsed with the loss of 35 lives. While rescuers tore at the rubble they heard a voice shout 'Heave awa' chaps, I'm no dead yet!' When they reached the survivor they found a young boy who later lived to a good age. His portrait and the words of his cry are to be seen above the entrance to the Close. Here also Sir William Fettes, wine and tea merchant and founder of Fettes College, had his shop. Down **Chalmers Close** (No 81 north) can be seen all that remains of the once magnificent Trinity College Church (just how magnificent can be seen in the Trinity College Altarpiece on loan to the National Gallery at the Mound). Demolished in 1848 to make room for Waverley Station, part of the Church was rebuilt in 1872 off Jeffrey Street.

## Museum of Childhood

The Museum of Childhood was created by the Edinburgh optician Patrick Murray (1908-81), Chairman of Edinburgh Corporation's Libraries and Museums Committee, out of a collection of his own toys, 'a pitiful handful of soldiers, building blocks and railway stuff'. The Museum, founded in 1955 and extended in 1986, was the first of its kind in the world.

**Hyndford Close** (No 34 south) was the mansion of the 3rd Earl of Hyndford (an ambassador to a number

of European courts during the War of Austrian
Succession, the Seven Years' War and the Jacobite
Rebellion). Jean Maxwell, Duchess of Gordon, as a
child went for water from the well outside **Fountain
Close**, riding on the back of a pig; she became a friend
of Burns when he came to Edinburgh and was the
centre of polite society. Professor Rutherford, the
inventor of the gas lamp and grandfather of Sir Walter
Scott, lived there, and in the Lodge St David Sir Walter
Scott himself became a Freemason.

Each Close is a cross-section of history: we come to
**Fountain Close** (No 22 south) where Thomas
Bassendyne produced the first printed Bible in
Scotland in 1574. Between 1704-81 The College of
Physicians had their premises in the Close and opened
a cold water bath for the use of the public. The well
which gave the Close its name has now been moved
over the High Street and to the east.

**Tweeddale Court** (No 14 south) was built in 1576
for Dame Margaret Kerr, daughter of the 1st Earl of
Lothian. Originally there was a garden there and an
avenue of lime-trees leading down to the Cowgate.
The building was modernised by Robert Adam and
two Doric columns added around 1799. Later it
became the head office of the British Linen Bank, and
in 1806 a Bank messenger named William Begbie was
murdered and robbed of £4392: part of the money
was found later but not the murderer. In 1817 the
publishing firm of Oliver & Boyd took over the
premises until 1973. Today the **Scottish Poetry Library** is
based there.

The last Close on the south side is the **World's End**,
so called because it was next to the **Netherbow Port**
which marked the boundary of the Old Town until the
Burgh of Canongate became part of Edinburgh in
1856.

**Moubray House** (today a private dwelling) is formed
from a 16th-century addition to a 15th-century base.
George Jamesone (1590-1644), the portrait painter,
had his studio on the upper floor (*see*: National
Portrait Gallery). In 1706 the English journalist Daniel
Defoe came to Edinburgh to spy for the Government
on the progress made by the Union of the Parliaments
and edited *The Edinburgh Courant* as a cover.

## John Knox Museum

A 15th-century house with outlook up the High Street from its timber balconies on the west side, and down the Canongate from its south-facing wooden galleries. The first recorded tenants of the house in 1525 were the Arres family. In 1556 Mariota Arres and her husband James Mossman, a jeweller, set up their home there. Mossman's father John was a goldsmith who had redesigned the Scottish Crown. In time James Mossman became Master of the Mint and Assayer to Mary Queen of Scots and was obliged to live at Edinburgh Castle where the Mint was located at that time. Mossman was eventually executed for having supported the Queen.

It has generally been believed that the great Scottish Reformer John Knox (1815-72), elected Minister of St Giles in 1559, was given the house as his manse up to his death. Today the house is owned by the Church of Scotland and preserved as a memorial to John Knox and the Reformation. At the projecting corner of the building is a sundial with a figure of the Prophet Moses pointing to a sunburst partly hidden in cloud and labelled 'God' in Greek and Latin (meaning that God is a mystery). Between 1839 and the early 1900s this sundial was covered by a miniature wooden pulpit with the figure of John Knox preaching (now displayed in the house).

The **Netherbow Arts Centre** (next door to the John Knox Museum) opened in 1972. Its presence is signalled by a bronze model of the Netherbow Port high above the entrance, the Netherbow Port Bell, and an old carving from the Port in the courtyard. The site of the narrow Netherbow Port is marked in the High Street by brass plates. Built in 1513 and damaged in 1544 by the Earl of Hertford, the Port had a tall steeple and was well fortified. On its walls the heads of criminals were stuck on spikes. The Port was demolished in 1764 to widen the road for traffic.

*The Netherbow Port (demolished in 1764) from the east, separating Edinburgh from the Canongate. Other Ports were the Cowgate, Bristo and West Port. The Ports were the main gateways into the city.*

## The City Art Centre

The City Art Centre was opened in Market Street in 1980 to house and display works from the City's Collection. The Collection owes its origin partly to a bequest from Miss Jean F Watson and to works belonging to the Scottish Modern Art Association which the City acquired in 1964. The Collection contains many paintings and drawings relating to Edinburgh.

# Canongate

Edinburgh owes its existence to the defensive advantages of the Castle Rock; the **Royal Burgh of Canongate**, on the other hand, was founded by David I in 1143 for peaceful religious purposes. The roles of the two burghs were complementary: the Sword and the Cross. It was not till 1856 that the Canongate reluctantly became part of Edinburgh.

Making a short detour south into **St Mary's Street** the visitor sees a plaque (above No 2) which records that this was the first building erected under the Improvement Act of 1867 directed by Lord Provost William Chambers.

A little further down the road is **Boyd's Entry** on the north wall of which is commemorated the arrival at Boyd's Inn of Dr Samuel Johnson on 14 August 1773 on the way to his Highland Tour. It was here that James Boswell found his distinguished visitor in a rage at a waiter who, instead of using silver tongs, had picked up a lump of sugar in his greasy fingers and dropped it into the Doctor's lemonade, upon which the latter hurled his glass out of the window!

Cross back to the Royal Mile and look north down **Jeffrey Street**: once this was Leith Wynd which ran in a straight line to Trinity College Church and Paul's Work below the Calton Rock where James Ballantyne printed the novels of Sir Walter Scott. It was down Leith Wynd also that the members of the Cape Club gingerly negotiated the bulge of the Netherbow Port after a night of good companionship.

At No 206 Canongate (south) a plaque honours the Master plumber George Chalmers (1773-1836) who left money to build Chalmers Hospital, while to the north the 'Moroccan' statuette high on the wall of **Mid Common Close** (No 293) is said to commemorate a highly romantic tale. Young Andrew Gray, son of the Lord Provost's brother-in-law, was to be executed for helping to burn down the Lord Provost's house during the street violence which followed the coronation of Charles I in 1633. Sentenced to death, Gray managed to escape from the Tolbooth, reached Leith and escaped abroad. Twelve years later Edinburgh was ravaged by the Plague. When the epidemic was at its worst an Algerian pirate ship was seen to anchor off Leith. Soon a strongly-armed detachment of pirates arrived at the Netherbow Port and threatened to attack if a large ransom was not handed over.

In reply the Provost gave his only daughter as security but pointed out that she was already ill with the Plague. The leader of the pirates promised to heal her. This he did in a house in the Canongate and then the pirate leader revealed himself as none other than Andrew Gray. He had fallen in love with the Provost's daughter and decided to spare the town the vengeance he had planned. The two were soon married and lived the remainder of their days in the Canongate. High on the wall above his house (No 273 **Morocco Land**) he placed a statue of his benefactor, the Emperor of Morocco (which was moved to Mid Common Close this century).

Robert Chambers has a different explanation: his version tells of a young Edinburgh woman who was kidnapped, taken abroad by an African slave-trader and sold to the Emperor of Morocco. From Morocco she wrote to her family and was able to arrange for her brother to trade between Africa and Edinburgh, so much so that his business prospered. In gratitude he erected a statue of the Emperor, wearing a turban and a necklace of precious stones.

**Chessel's Court** (No 240 south), first built around 1748, was the scene of the unmasking of Deacon Brodie in 1787 when he attempted to rob the Excise Office there. He had visited the Office, made impressions of the keys and memorised the layout of the building. The robbery took place on 5 March and all that Brodie and his gang managed to steal was £16. Soon afterwards one of his accomplices turned King's Evidence but Brodie had escaped to the Continent. He was eventually captured and executed at the west end of the Old Tolbooth (at the third attempt). His double life is said to have inspired Stevenson to write *Dr Jekyll and Mr Hyde*.

To the north is **New Street** where Lord Kames (1696-1782), Lord of Session, author of books on law and philosophy, and an agricultural improver, lived at the top on the east side. Further east down the Canongate is **Jack's Land** where David Hume lived

from 1753-62 and finished his *History of England*.
Also here, the elderly Countess of Eglinton entertained
Bonnie Prince Charlie in 1745.

Behind was the mansion of the fearsome General
Tam Dalyell of the Binns (c.1599-1685) who had
trained as a soldier in the Russian army fighting the
Turks. He crushed the Covenanter army at Rullion
Green in 1666; in 1681 he raised the Royal Scots
Greys. General Dalyell had stopped shaving his beard
as a protest at the execution of Charles I, so that in time
it reached down almost to his waist!

**Old Playhouse Close** (No 196 south) once housed a
flourishing theatre, the foundation-stone of which was
laid by John Ryan, a well-known Covent Garden ac-
tor. The theatre opened in 1747 (putting a rival
establishment in the Tailors Hall out of business). The
first performance of the Rev. John Home's tragedy
*Douglas* took place there in 1756, whose success
inspired the legendary shout from the audience of
'Whaur's your Wullie Shakespeare noo!'

When the spanking new Theatre Royal opened at
the east end of Princes Street in 1769 the fortunes of
the Old Playhouse rapidly declined. The poet Robert
Fergusson (himself not buried far away in Greyfriars
Kirk) viewed the ruins of the theatre with regret:

'No more, from box to box, the basket, piled
With oranges as radiant as the spheres,
Shall with their luscious virtues charm the sense
Of taste and smell. Oh! look here,
Upon this roofless and forgotten pile.'

In front of Old Playhouse Close was **St John's Cross**,
used for proclamations and other ceremonial events
(such as the knighting of the Lord Provost by Charles I
in 1633).

On the south side of the Canongate in **St John's
Pend** the Knights of the Order of St John had their
houses and today their Priory is still on the same site.
Tobias Smollett (1721-71), the novelist, stayed in the
Pend with his sister Mrs Telfer on the first floor in 1753
and also while writing *Humphrey Clinker* in the
summer of 1766. The Canongate Kilwinning Lodge
Hall (built in 1736 and thought to be the oldest

Masonic lodge-room in the world) was visited by Burns in 1786. He was affiliated on 1 February, and on 1 March 1787 the title of Poet Laureate was conferred on Burns.

**'Shoemakers Land'** (No 197 north) once contained the Hall of the Incorporation of Cordiners (Shoemakers), built in 1682. In front of the building can be seen a panel with the Cordiner's rounding or paring knife and the Crown of St Crispin (*see*: Huntly House Museum) with the observation that 'Blessed is he that wisely doth the poor man's case consider'.

**'Bible Land'** (No 185) next door dates from 1677 and is so called from the two quotations from the Bible: 'Behold how good a thing it is and how becoming well together such as brethren are in unity to dwell' (Psalm 133) and 'It is an honour for a man to cease from strife' (Proverbs XX, 3).

The **Canongate Tolbooth** (built in 1591 on the site of the Auld Tolbuith) had the same functions as Edinburgh's. An inscription to James VI reads: 'Justice and Religion are a Ruler's strongest weapons'. The Canongate arms can also be seen: a stag's head with a cross caught in its antlers and the words 'This is the way to Paradise'. The Tolbooth will shortly house a new museum – 'The People's Story'.

**Moray House** (No 174 south) was built around 1628 by the Dowager Countess of Home, an Englishwoman (her initials 'MH' – Mary Home – can be seen on various parts of the building). At her death in 1645 the house passed to her daughter Margaret, Countess of Moray. Both Charles I and the Marquis of Argyll stayed in the house. In the summer of 1648 Oliver Cromwell made Moray House his headquarters and it is said that while there he revealed to the Covenanters his plan to execute Charles I. After the Battle of Dunbar in 1650 Cromwell again spent some time there.

On 18 May, soon after the wedding of the daughter of the 4th Earl of Argyle, the chief guests are said to have assembled on the balcony of Moray House to see the Marquis of Montrose tied to a cart and carried to the Parliament House to receive the death sentence. Montrose was hanged at the Mercat Cross on 21 May. Only a year later the Earl of Argyle himself suffered the same fate.

During the negotiations for the Treaty of Union between England and Scotland in 1707 the signatures of the Scottish Lords were put to the Treaty in the Pavilion of Moray House (still there in dilapidated condition). Moray House was leased to the British Linen Company in 1753, who filled it with staplers, spinners, weavers, packers and carters. From 1791-92 it was occupied by Duncan Cowan, a paper-maker, and today it has had a long and influential history as a College of Education.

## Huntly House Museum
*(No 146 The Canongate)*

Originally three small houses which were joined in 1570, Huntly House (so called because the Duchess of Gordon had a flat there in the middle of the 18th century) was bought by the Incorporation of Hammermen who owned it till 1762.

Known as 'The Speaking House', its Canongate front has copies of three inscriptions (the originals are inside):

1 'Today it's me, tomorrow you. Worrying doesn't achieve anything.'
2 'Just as you decide what to say, so I choose what to listen to.'
3 'A well-balanced person takes the long-term view.'

When the building was restored in 1932 two others were added:

4 'In old age I grow young.' (TBW= Sir T Whitson, Lord Provost).
5 'There is new hope of life.' (Carved blades of corn growing out of human bones).

Today Huntly House explores these themes as the main local history museum in Edinburgh, preserving what is best from the past in order to help us come to terms with the present.

Below Huntly House is **Acheson House** (No 146 south) formerly the mansion of Sir Archibald Acheson of Abercairny (Secretary of State for Scotland in the time of Charles I) and of his wife Dame Margaret Hamilton. Sir Archibald became a Lord of Session in 1625 just after the accession of Charles I and three years later bought one of the baronetcies of Nova Scotia (sasine to which was given with a piece of earth from the Castle Esplanade). The family crest of the Achesons can be seen from Bakehouse Close on the west side of the house: a cock standing on a trumpet with the motto 'Vigilantibus'. After a number of years variously occupied (including a period as a house of ill repute) Acheson House was restored in 1937 and opened as the **Scottish Craft Centre** in 1952.

*The Cock and Trumpet crest (Acheson House).*

**Bakehouse Close** is worth looking at for the timber cladding and the contrasting textures of harling (Scottish pebble-dash), dressed stone (ashlar) and rubble walls which give a good indication of the uninhibited changes in construction techniques over the centuries.

Across the road is the **Canongate Kirk** built in 1688 to accommodate the congregation of the Canongate when James VII threw them out of Holyrood (their traditional parish church) in order to convert the Abbey Church into a Roman Catholic Chapel for the Knights of the Thistle (*see*: Holyroodhouse). In 1745 Bonnie Prince Charlie's prisoners from the Battle of Prestonpans were held in the Canongate Kirk. In the grounds of Canongate Kirk is the Canongate Mercat Cross which stood from 1128 to 1888 just in front of what is now the main gate of the church. The octagonal shaft is 16th-century and the capital and head date from 1888.

Among the famous people buried in the Canongate churchyard are the poet Robert Fergusson, George Drummond (founder of the New Town), Professor James Gregory (inventor of 'Gregory's Mixture', the popular medicine), Nancy Craig (Mrs Maclehose – the 'Clarinda' of Robert Burns' 'Sylvander'), Dugald Stewart, Adam Smith and the musician Johann F Lampe (Handel's favourite bassoonist).

The Canongate Manse at **Reid's Court** dates from 1690, originally built as a coaching-inn and named after James Reid, a coachmaker. The house was used as a manse from 1789 to 1832 and was restored again in 1958.

**Panmure House** is a 17th-century building (now only accessible from Little Lochend Close). The economist Adam Smith, author of *The Wealth of Nations*, lived in Panmure House (1778-90) and died there. Smith had come to Edinburgh from Kirkcaldy in 1778 as a Commissioner of Customs.

At Brown's Close (No 65 north) is **Golfer's Land**, once the home of John Paterson (whose grandfather had lived there from 1601). A plaque tells the story of the game of golf Paterson played with the Duke of York around 1681 (*see*: Huntly House Museum). The coat of arms above the plaque shows a hand holding a golf-club over a helmet with the legend 'Far and Sure'. A notice refers to a Latin inscription on the east-facing wall of the garden behind. Said to have been written by Dr Archibald Pitcairne, it reads: 'When Paterson who, in succession to nine ancestors who had been champions, himself won the championship in the

Scots' own game, he began to build up this house from the ground, which all alone produced so many champions.' Then the anagram of John *Patersone* follows: 'I hate no person'.

**Jenny Hall's Change House** which flourished from 1600-1857 was famous for claret drawn from the butt and for the gelatinous Younger's Ale (*see*: plaque in Whitefoord House). The tavern was the meeting-place of the English poet John Gay (1685-1732) and Allan Ramsay. Gay, the author of *The Beggar's Opera*, stayed for a few weeks in 1729 at Queensberry House.

**Whitefoord House** was for long the home of Professor Dugald Stewart (1753-1828), Professor of Moral Philosophy at Edinburgh University. Today it is a residence for Scottish War Veterans.

On the south side (No 64) stands **Queensberry House** built in 1682 by William, 1st Duke of Queensberry who wielded enormous power in the reign of Charles II and was Lord High Commissioner early in the reign of James VII. The Duke helped to put William of Orange on the throne. He was a great miser but an extravagant builder of houses; and although illiterate – he dictated all his letters to a secretary – he was a great collector of books.

A horrific story is told about the son of the 2nd Duke of Queensberry (one of the principal architects of the Union of the Parliaments in 1707). His son was mentally handicapped but extremely strong and very tall, and was kept hidden away in a room with boarded-up windows in Queensberry House. On the day that the Treaty of Union was signed, the son's keeper left the room to look at the rioting crowds in the Canongate; when he returned he found to his horror the Duke's son sitting in the kitchen roasting the kitchen-boy on a spit!

The Earl of March (known as 'Old Q') was a sporting man who spent much of his fortune on drink and entertainment. He sold Queensberry House to the Government in 1801. In 1808 it was used as a barracks and then as a house of refuge for the destitute. Today Queensberry House is a hospital.

**White Horse Close** (No 31 north) was restored in 1889 and 1964. In the 1500s it was the location of the Royal Mews; in 1623 Laurence Ord, a merchant, built the White Horse Inn and coaching stables and named them after Mary Queen of Scots' favourite white palfrey. When a coach service was introduced, the Newcastle coach left from the back entrance of the Inn. In 1745 Jacobite officers used the Inn as their headquarters and in 1793 William Dick (1793-1866), son of a farrier and founder of the Edinburgh Veterinary School (popularly known as the 'Dick Vet'), was born here.

**Lothian House** (known as 'Lothian Hut') was the town house of the Marquis of Lothian. For a time it was the home of Professor Dugald Stewart (whose pupils included Lord Brougham and Lord Palmerston). In 1825 it was demolished. The **Girth Cross** was where the traffic roundabout now stands: it was the boundary of the Abbey Sanctuary where proclamations and executions took place (Lady Warriston, for example, was executed there in 1600 by the 'Maiden' (guillotine) for plotting to kill her husband).

Formerly the Royal Tennis Court was located outside the **Water Gate** (opposite the entrance to Calton Road). Here in 1682 the Duke of York held the first of his many revels, an event which was a turning-point in the musical life of the City. Behind the Tennis Court were the Physic Gardens, one of the predecessors of the present Royal Botanic Garden.

Finally, we come to the curious building known as **'Queen Mary's Bath-house'**, but more probably a summer-house. Originally the house stood at the edge of the Physic Gardens but the construction of the north gate involved the driving of a roadway through the Gardens and so the 'Bath-house' was left high and dry.

# The Palace of Holyroodhouse

## Early Visitors

The Palace has its origins in the monastery guest-house which stood to the west of the Abbey Church. Here visitors (the Kings of Scotland among them) would stay, in peaceful surroundings in the shadow of the hills. From time to time events of major importance would bring visitors of standing to the Abbey guest-house. In 1177, for example, the Papal Legate Vivian held a Council at the Abbey; in 1189 the nobles and prelates of Scotland met at Holyrood to discuss the ransom for William the Lion, and in 1326 King Robert I ('Robert the Bruce') held a Parliament there. In 1328 the Treaty of Edinburgh (which recognised Robert I and his heirs as Kings of Scotland) was ratified at the Abbey of Holyrood. By hosting such national events the Abbey of Holyroodhouse inevitably became a convenient occasional royal residence.

King David II was the first Scottish monarch to be buried at the Abbey (1370), but it is with James II that Holyrood receives the seal of royal approval: he was born, crowned, married and buried (1460) there. Another royal celebration took place at Holyrood in 1469 when Margaret (c.1457-86), daughter of Christian I of Denmark and Norway and wife of James III, was crowned Queen of Scotland.

*Holyrood Palace.*

## A Renaissance Palace

First mention of a 'Royal chamber' comes in 1473 and in 1501 James IV began the construction of an exclusively royal residence of some size in preparation for his marriage (1503) to Margaret Tudor, daughter of Henry VII of England, celebrated by the poet William Dunbar in his 'The Thistle and the Rose' and accompanied by jousting, feasting and dancing.

The new Palace was built on the site of the outer court of the monastery and probably involved adaptation of existing structures as well as fresh building. The present north-west tower, turreted and built to withstand attack, with gunloops and battlements, was begun during this period, while the rest of the Palace occupied the ground running south.

## Destruction and Restoration

Construction was paralleled by destruction: in 1569 the east part of the Abbey Church was demolished by order of the General Assembly of the Church of Scotland (as in 1688 a furious mob was to ransack the Catholic Chapel Royal and the Jesuit College established by James VII, breaking into the Royal Vaults in the process).

For the home-coming of James VI and I the Palace was enthusiastically refurbished (as the wall paintings in Mary Queen of Scots' bedroom indicate). When Charles I came to the Abbey to be crowned in 1633 a similar redecoration took place. A less amicable welcome awaited him on his return in 1641, following his attempt to impose bishops on the Church of Scotland.

Oliver Cromwell billeted his troops at Holyrood in 1651 and not long after, the royal apartments were damaged by fire. Cromwell, however, was aware of the importance of the Palace and rebuilding and extension took place in 1658-59.

It was with the Restoration that major reconstruction was started. Charles II ( who had been in Edinburgh in 1650) approved plans to rebuild the north, east and south sides of the main court, and the inscription marking the construction of a handsome piazza can still be seen today with the name of the Master Mason, Robert Mylne, carved into the stone.

## Symbol of Past Glories

Since the Union of the Crowns in 1603 when James VI and I left Edinburgh to take up residence in his new capital of London, the importance of Edinburgh as a political centre declined. From the Union of Parliaments in 1707 this trend became irreversible. Holyrood was now a private lodging for noblemen, or housed colourful relics of a deposed monarchy (Charles X of France who occupied the west part of the Palace from 1796 to 1803). The Palace glittered briefly in 1745 when Prince Charles Edward Stuart held a magnificent soirée and raised hopes which were never to be fulfilled.

A less romantic but more tangible impression was left by the slightly absurd figure of the Hanoverian George IV gorgeously dressed for the glens and the heather, accepting the Honours of Scotland (the Crown, the Sceptre and Sword of State) and entertaining 2000 members of the aristocracy in 1822, the whole stage-managed with flair by Sir Walter Scott. George IV ordered the repair of the Palace and this gave new life to Holyrood as a colourful setting for the monarch, and as a symbol for the nation.

When Queen Victoria first came to Holyrood twenty years later she began a long tradition of royal visits which led to its refurbishment into a comfortable royal residence. King George V and Queen Mary also played their part in the regeneration of the Palace (most evident in the Throne Room with its two red thrones). King George VI and Queen Elizabeth are commemorated by a portrait of the Queen Mother. The present Royal Family has kept up the habit of regular visits to Holyrood.

## The Abbey Sanctuary

The right of 'sanctuary' at Holyrood derived from the foundation charter of David I. In earlier days the Canons of Holyrood subjected aristocratic seekers after sanctuary to ordeal by fire and the lowly-born to ordeal by water. In later times abuses crept in: criminals were admitted to sanctuary who should have suffered punishment in the civil courts. In 1532 the Scottish Court of Session came into being and shortly afterwards the Scottish Parliament passed an Act compelling church sanctuaries to send offenders to the civil courts.

The boundaries of the **Royal Sanctuary of Holyrood** included the whole of the Royal Park, from Salisbury Crags down to Duddingston Loch, the south of Abbeyhill, Dumbiedykes and even the crest of Arthur's Seat. Within this territory, in houses to the east of the Palace and near the **Girth Cross** (the visible symbol of Sanctuary, placed in the centre of the junction at the foot of the Canongate – now a roundabout) lived the so-called 'Abbey Lairds'.

William Chambers (1800-83), while a young bookseller's apprentice, was appointed to sell lottery tickets to the inmates: 'The Sanctuary, which embraced a cluster of decayed buildings in front and on both sides of Holyrood Palace was, at that time, seldom without distinguished characters from England – some of them gaunt, oldish gentlemen, seemingly broken-down men of fashion, wearing big gold spectacles, who now drew out existence here in defiance of creditors.'

Dr Peter Morris described 'a variety of little miserable patchwork dwellings' from which the inmates anxiously scrutinised strangers.

## A Modern Sanctuary

A sanctuary of a different kind exists today where murderers or debtors once sheltered from civil justice and the punishments of the law courts. It is possible to read into the legend of the foundation a warning against over-hunting and a call for conservation of natural resources. In the polluted air of a modern city green belts are vital for health. The **Queen's Park** today is a haven for flora and fauna, and has achieved a more lasting international importance in providing proof to the 'father of modern Geology', James Hutton (1726-97), that the earth's surface was not formed by the action of the sea but by volcanic activity. This Hutton was able to demonstrate in his *Theory of the Earth* (1785) which was in great part based on his observation of the rock formations of the Salisbury Crags.

# SOUTHSIDE

Starting from the western end of the area of Edinburgh immediately south of the Castle we encounter two time-honoured homes of drama and music which have provided entertainment to the public. The **Royal Lyceum** in Grindlay Street held over 2500 people on the opening night – 10 September 1883 – when Henry Irving and Ellen Terry performed a scene from Shakespeare's *Much Ado About Nothing*, and the managers, Messrs Howard and Wyndham, declaimed rhyming verses from the stage.

Beside the Lyceum Theatre is the circular, copper-domed **Usher Hall** (1914), built with a donation of £100 000 from the brewer Andrew Usher, which holds 2900 people. Here all the greatest names in the world of music have performed – soloists, orchestra and conductors.

Not far away at Leven Street is the **King's Theatre**, opened in 1906, with its voluptuous plasterwork and statuary round the boxes beside the stage. The King's, like the Lyceum, has played host to the 'stars' and, unlike the Lyceum, has staged opera from the finest companies, as well as music hall and variety.

Our route now takes us south up Lady Lawson Street to Lauriston Place.

# Lothian and Borders Fire Brigade

In the Headquarters of the Brigade, located at Lauriston Place, the **James Braidwood Room** and other memorabilia record the growth of the fire service in the City. From 1681 there had been fire-points attached to the water-pipe running from the Castle to the public wells. Edinburgh had special problems, with its sudden steep gradients, and many of its houses as high as 15 storeys (it was not till 1698 that the Scottish Parliament limited the number of storeys to five).

It was not till the fire of February 1700 that the Town Council began to take steps to combat the danger of fire. This was the worst fire in Edinburgh since 1544 when the English under the Earl of Hertford had destroyed many parts of the town. In 1700 the fire spread over Parliament Close and almost 200 families were made homeless.

An Act of 1703 ordered the appointment of twelve firemasters with six assistants each, who were to be provided with a leather cap, a large axe, a sledge-hammer and handsaw. Some 300 leather buckets and other equipment were to be stored at various strategic points throughout the town. Every tenement had to have supplies of rope and water in case of fire. Fortunately there were no serious fires in Edinburgh till 1771 when a large fire broke out in the Lawnmarket.

**The Great Fire of Edinburgh** (see: Huntly House Museum) broke out in a printer's shop in the High Street before 10 pm on 15 November 1824. Although several companies were on the scene shortly afterwards, by midnight four tenements were blazing. At midday on the following day the steeple of the Tron Kirk was on fire; the bell melted and molten metal showered down on to the High Street.

It grew dark and by now the fire had spread to Parliament Square; by 5 am on the next day most of the eastern side of the Square was burnt or was blazing. It was not till the morning of 19 November that a sudden downpour of rain put an end to the fire.

Fighting the flames had been James Braidwood, the young Firemaster, with his 'Pioneers' (mainly seamen or craftsmen). Braidwood was the son of an Edinburgh cabinet-maker, educated at the High School, trained as a surveyor, and had had some experience in the police. When he took over as Firemaster he used to train his men at 4 am to give them experience of working in darkness.

The Edinburgh Fire Brigade was divided into four areas: East (Fishmarket Close – red helmets), West (Fountainbridge – blue), North (Rose Street – yellow) and South (Teviot Place – grey).

Braidwood did not shirk from danger: while in Edinburgh, for example, he removed a large quantity of gunpowder from a burning shop. He died in London where, as Master of the London Fire Engine Establishment, he was directing operations at a fire in Tooley Street close to London Bridge. Braidwood's axe and breast-badge are on view at Brigade Headquarters as well as a copy of his book *Fire Prevention and Fire Extinction* (1886), his bosun's pipe for signalling to his men, and prints of his funeral procession to Abney Park Cemetery, London.

# The Royal Infirmary of Edinburgh

The Infirmary, like the New Town, was very much the brainchild of George Drummond, Edinburgh's dynamic and far-sighted Lord Provost who had a genius for finance and fund-raising.

In 1729 a 'hospital for the destitute sick' was opened in Robertson's Close (in what is now Infirmary Street): it had a mere six beds. Nine years later the foundation-stone of the first Infirmary was laid facing Infirmary Street. The new Royal Infirmary (designed by William Adam) was completed in 1747 with four storeys and a fifth storey in the centre to house an operating-theatre with tiered seating.

Adam's Infirmary was demolished in 1884: one north-west pavilion remains at the Old Surgical Hospital in Drummond Street as well as the gate-piers of the Infirmary. The giant scrolls which once supported the Infirmary's facade are now built into either side of a bungalow in Redford Road while further up the road Ionic half-columns have been joined to create the Covenanters Monument. The

49

statue of George II as a victorious Roman general stands outside the main entrance to the present Infirmary.

David Bryce's new Royal Infirmary was constructed between 1872 and 1879. In 1881 a number of panels recording donations to the Infirmary were transferred to the new building. From them we learn that in 1745 the Islands of Barbados gave £180, Antigua £143 and Jamaica £1500. In 1776 David Hume the philosopher died and left £50; £400 were given from a share in the profits of the 1815 Musical Festival; Grand Duke Michael of Russia gave £50 in 1818 and in the next year the Musical Festival gave another £100 and the Caledonian Hunt contributed £50. At the time of his visit in 1822 George IV gave £120 and the 'Swedish Nightingale', the soprano Jenny Lind (Mrs Goldschmidt), who performed at the Music Hall in George Street, gave £157.

Edward Prince of Wales laid the foundation-stone of the new Royal Infirmary in Lauriston Place. In 1879 subscriptions for wood furnishings were received from: Ladies of Edinburgh (£552), North British Railway officials and servants (£446), Pupils of Edinburgh (£336), A Widow (£200), Commercial Travellers (£210), Hotelkeepers of Edinburgh and Neighbourhood (£300).

The list of eminent surgeons and physicians who have trained, taught or practised at the Royal Infirmary is too long to detail in full. Edinburgh's reputation in medical research and innovation would have been impossible without the University or the Infirmary, one inextricably connected to the other – research being meaningless without the everyday spur of human suffering (which the Infirmary and Edinburgh's many other hospitals exist to alleviate).

Of the illustrious names connected with the Royal Infirmaries of Edinburgh these are the most famous: Alexander Monro Primus (founder of the Edinburgh School of Medicine), Monro Secundus and Tertius, James Syme (the Napoleon of Surgery), James Young Simpson (the discoverer of the anaesthetic properties of chloroform), Henry Littlejohn (Edinburgh's first Medical Officer of Health), Joseph Lister (pioneer of antisepsis), and Sir Robert Philip (the conqueror of tuberculosis).

The magnificent **George Heriot's School** across the road was completed around 1700, the result of an endowment by the banker and jeweller of James VI to build a school for needy children of Edinburgh burgesses.

The gardens of the school were used by the Italian balloonist Vincenzo Lunardi (1787) to make an ascent over the Forth to Fife; the Defensive Bands drilled there at the time of the Napoleonic Wars. Among its famous former pupils were the portrait painter Sir Henry Raeburn who came as an orphan in 1764. Heriot's has also founded seven other schools in the City for the sons of burgesses.

When the English poet Robert Southey visited the school in 1819 he gave this description of mealtime: 'As soon as they had done, four strapping women came in, bearing two large wooden tubs; they went to the cross table at the head of the hall, and two going right, two left caught up the tin porridge cups and toss'd them into the tubs, making the noblest noise I ever heard as an accompaniment to a dinner. Then after the grace, the urchins went, to the time of their own footsteps, two and two, scuffling over the sanded floor.'

Immediately next to Heriot's is **Greyfriars Kirk**, which dates from the grant in 1562 to the town by Mary Queen of Scots. It was built in the garden of Greyfriars monastery in order to accommodate the growing congregation of the parish church of Edinburgh – St Giles High Kirk. Many of the town's greatest men and women were buried in the church-yard and many 'paupers' (the poet William McGonagall for example) or criminals (such as captain Porteous of the Porteous Riots) or disgraced political figures such as the 4th Earl of Morton, sentenced to death for complicity in the murders of Rizzio and Darnley. It was here also that the momentous National Covenant was signed in 1638 against English ways of worship.

# The National Museum of Scotland
*(Royal Museum, Chambers Street)*

The foundation-stone of the Museum was laid by

Prince Albert in 1861 only two months before his death. Its distinctive feature was that it was a comprehensive museum built round Edinburgh University's Natural History Museum and a new Industrial Museum.

Among material acquired by the Museum was the fossil collection of Hugh Miller (1802-56), the Playfair collection of scientific instruments, weapons, tools and costumes from traders of the Hudson's Bay Company, items sent back from Africa by the missionary David Livingstone (1813-73) and the collection of arms and armour made by the artist Sir Joseph Noel Paton (1821-1907).

# Surgeons Hall
*(Nicolson Street)*

In 1505 the **Royal College of Surgeons** was founded by James IV from the Guild of Barber-Surgeons. The earliest Museum of the Surgeons dates from at least 1699 when the Guild advertised for 'natural and artificial curiosities'. Only two such 'curiosities' remain: a dissection by Archibald Pitcairne (1652-1713) dated 1702 and one of 1718 by Alexander Monro I (1697-1767). Alexander Monro III (1773-1859) was Professor both of Anatomy and Surgery. His lectures in Anatomy amounted to little more than the word-for-word repetition of the lecture-notes of his grandfather Alexander Monro I and he never practised surgery himself.

Pressure came from the Royal College to separate the teaching of Anatomy from that of Surgery. The University of Edinburgh refused to do so and accordingly the College appointed its own Professor of Surgery in 1804, one of his responsibilities being the care of a Museum as an important resource for the teaching of Surgery.

In 1832 a new Surgeons Hall was completed, designed by W H Playfair as an imposing Greek temple. During this period (1826-31) Dr Robert Knox had been Conservator of the Museum. He also provided a very popular and successful course of lectures in Anatomy and brought the catalogue of the Anatomical Museum up to date. His achievement, however, was marred by the scandal in 1828 when, by chance, the 'body-snatchers' Burke and Hare decided to deliver their murdered victims to Dr Knox for dissection.

# Edinburgh University

Edinburgh University was unique in Scotland in being the first Post-Reformation university and in having been founded, not by the Church, but by the Town Council. The University was known as 'The Tounis College' and in 1617 achieved the status of 'King James' University'.

The first Regent (Principal) in 1583 was Robert Rollock, a 28-year-old scholar from Stirling. Students were aged 16 to 19 at that time and the graduates of the University have from time immemorial been 'capped' with 'the Seat of Learning' – 'Geordie Buchanan's breeks', the original trousers of the Reformation scholar and teacher George Buchanan, who is buried in Greyfriars churchyard. The University of Edinburgh can boast two Nobel Prizewinners: Professor Charles Glover Barkla (Professor of Natural Philosophy 1913-22) and the former Principal the late Sir Edward Appleton. Their awards were made for their work in revealing the nature of X-radiation and in Physics respectively.

In the field of Politics the University has also been influential. Prime Ministers Palmerston and Russell were educated mainly in Edinburgh. Sir Alfred Ewing, Principal of the University, enabled the United States to decipher the Zimmerman telegram in which the German Foreign Secretary of that name encouraged Mexico to attack the USA in 1917, infuriating American opinion and speeding up the USA's entry into the war.

Among distinguished Edinburgh graduates in Politics have been: Baroness Lee, John Selwyn-Lloyd, Dr Hastings Banda (President of Malawi) and Lord Pitt of Hampstead (the first coloured member of the House of Lords).

Past Rectors of the University include: William Gladstone (1859), Thomas Carlyle (1865), David Lloyd George (1920), Stanley Baldwin (1932) and Winston Churchill (1929). Two actors, Alistair Sim (1948) and James Robertson Justice (1957 and 1963) and the television pundit, Malcolm Muggeridge (who resigned sensationally from the pulpit of St Giles in 1968) have also held the office.

As early as 1858 Edinburgh University received the first African student, James Africanus Beale (born 1835 in Sierra Leone), who graduated as doctor in 1859. After becoming an MRCS of London, he was appointed Staff Assistant Surgeon in the Army, serving in the Gold Coast, working for 20 years, one of the first African doctors and one of the first African regular army officers.

The outside of the **Old Quad** of the University in South Bridge is by Robert Adam (1789), and the inside by William Playfair. The Old Quad is surrounded with history: where South College Street meets the South Bridge was once the site of the Kirk o' Field, ripped apart by an explosion when Darnley was murdered in 1567. North of the Old Quad is Guthrie Street where Sir Walter Scott was born in 1771.

The large and imposing dome topped by the 'Golden Boy' carrying the torch of Learning is by Rowand Anderson. Other 20th-century parts of the University are to be found in the tower-blocks of George Square.

At the east end of Chambers Street is **Adam House** which belongs to the University and contains, among other premises, the Adam House Theatre. In the foyer two plaques remind the visitor that the house of the Adam family stood on the site 'who by their work and genius did much to enhance the fame of their country and this University' and that it was at a later date also the site of an Operetta House.

The playwright Oliver Goldsmith as a medical student in 1752 lived in the High Street. From 1825-27 Charles Darwin (1809-82) and his brother Erasmus were students at the University and lodged on the fourth floor of No 11 **Lothian Street** which runs behind the Chambers Street Museum and the Old Quad.

Darwin collected specimens in the tidal pools on the shore of the Firth of Forth and managed to sail to sea with the fishermen of Newhaven to find specimens in their oyster-nets.

At No 46 the writer Thomas De Quincey (1785-1859) came in 1856 to contribute to *Blackwood's Magazine*. De Quincey, addicted to opium, tired out by his labours with the pen, used to fall asleep late at night and his landlady would often have to put out the flames when the dripping candle ignited the papers piled high on his desk and were even beginning to consume the sleeping author!

Walking south across **Bristo Square** we come to the **McEwan Hall** (completed in 1897), the work of Rowand Anderson and financed by Sir William McEwan, MP for the Central Division of Edinburgh (and chairman of the well-known Edinburgh firm of brewers). South of the Hall a bust and inscription records the site of the house where Archibald Campbell Tait (1811-82) was born. He succeeded Dr Arnold as the headmaster of Rugby School and was Archbishop of Canterbury from 1868 to his death.

Inside the Hall is a bronze bust (1898) of Sir William McEwan MP by Pittendrigh MacGillivray (1856-1938). To the left side of the stage is a roundel with a profile of Sir Walter Scott (aged 17) and the exhortation 'Watch Weel'; on the right is Thomas Carlyle (aged 20) and 'Work and Despair not'.

Behind the McEwan Hall is **George Square**, only two sides of which have escaped demolition at the hands of the University planners. Henry Erskine (1746-1817), Lord Advocate, lived either at No 24 or No 26. Cockburn remembers him as 'A tall and rather slender figure, a face sparkling with vivacity, a clear, sweet voice, and a general suffusion of elegance.'

At No 25 Sir Walter Scott lived (1774-97), fighting in the streets or on the grass of the Meadows with the boys of Bristo Street and Potterrow. A swelling in his ankle, the result of polio, made it sometimes difficult to go out (in spite of his strapping frame and muscular build) and he would sit in his room reading. He walked the two miles to a friend's house in Princes Street by seven in the morning in order to study with him. In his room at George Square the young student had 'more

books than shelves; a small painted cabinet with Scots
and Roman coins in it; a claymore, a Lochaber axe
mounted guard on a little print of Prince Charlie.'

Sometimes Scott went to the dancing assemblies
and noted that 'It was a proud night with me when I
first found that a pretty young woman could think it
worth her while to sit and talk with me hour after hour,
in a corner of the ball-room, while all the world were
capering in our view.' Sir Arthur Conan Doyle lived at
No 23 from the age of 17 to 21 (1876-80) when he was
a medical student at Edinburgh, while across the grass
was Dr Alexander Adam (1741-1809) who stayed at
No 39 on the east side. He was the Rector of the High
School and a distinguished writer on Roman
antiquities. Scott recalls that Adam's style of teaching
was neither rigid nor silent; 'His "noisy mansion"
which to others would have been a melancholy
bedlam, was the pride of his heart.' He suffered a
stroke and then died some few days later, his last
words being 'But it grows dark – the boys may
dismiss.'

At No 45 was Robert Jameson (1772-1854),
Professor of Natural History. Known as 'the father of
modern natural history', he experimented with
taxidermy (stuffed animals) at school and collected
specimens on the shore at Leith. He set up a network
of contacts and collector all over the world who sent
back material from Africa, Australia, the Pacific and
from Polar expeditions to the University's Natural
History Museum (which in 1854 became part of
Scotland's National Museum).

Robert Blair (1741-1811), Lord President of
Session, died at No 56. Lord Cockburn remembers
that 'He had been in Court that day, apparently in
good health, and had gone to take his usual walk from
his house in George Square round by Bruntsfield Links
and the Grange, where his solitary figure had long
been a known and respected object, when he was
struck by sudden illness, staggered home, and died.'

Henry Dundas, 1st Viscount Melville (1742-1811),
Lord Advocate, MP for Midlothian and known as
'Harry the Ninth, uncrowned King of Scotland', died
in the home of his nephew, Lord Chief Baron Dundas
at No 57 on the north-east side of the Square. Lord

Melville had come to Edinburgh for the funeral of Lord President Blair who died in the house next door: so the two friends lay dead with only a wall separating them.

Robert Dundas of Arniston also lived at No 57 (1819). The son of a Lord Advocate and grandson of another, he was 'in public affairs the most important person in this country', says Cockburn, 'for he was Lord Advocate in the most alarming times.' Robert Dundas was 'a little, alert, handsome, gentleman-like man, with a countenance and air beaming with sprightliness and gaiety, and dignified by considerable fire.'

Admiral Adam Duncan, 1st Viscount Camperdown (1731-1804), also lived on the north side of George Square on the site of what later became George Watson's Ladies College. Although most of the north side of the Square was demolished, the Admiral's house remains, with 'Admiral Duncan's Kitchen', and is now the Department of Psychology.

In 1792 a furious mob appeared in front of the house of the Admiral's neighbour, Dundas, protesting at his opposition to the moves to reform the electoral system. A straw dummy of Dundas was held up on a pole and set alight. This enraged the 61-year-old Admiral (who was still tall and immensely strong). He seized a crutch belonging to old Lady Dundas and, in the words of John Kay's *Portraits*, he rushed out of the house and 'laid about him among the crowd with great vigour; and even after the head of the crutch had been demolished, he continued to use the staff, until compelled to retreat by the overwhelming inequality of numbers.' Five years later, after Duncan's naval victory over the Dutch at Camperdown, a brigade of volunteers (around 2500 men) marched into George Square in slow time up to his house. The Viscount saluted the cavalry, infantry and the naval carriage draped with his flag. When they reached the North Bridge the crowd unhitched the horses from his carriage and pulled it through the New Town. At night the Lord Provost and Magistrates entertained Viscount Duncan at Fortune's Tavern in the High Street and presented him with the Freedom of the City.

# Charles Street

Beyond George Square, to the east, is Charles Street where (in No 7) Francis Jeffrey (1773-1850) was born. Jeffrey as a 13-year-old had seen Robert Burns in an Edinburgh Street and was impressed by the dark and flashing eye of the poet. Jeffrey was an advocate (Lord Advocate in 1830) but in October 1802 in his flat nearby on the third floor of Buccleuch Place, he and a number of his friends founded the Whig *Edinburgh Review* which he edited and to which he was to contribute more than 200 articles.

Jeffrey later bought and restored Craigcrook Castle where he would entertain friends in the garden. Jeffrey had spent some time at Oxford and had developed 'a high-keyed accent and a sharp pronunciation'. As Lord Advocate he took some of the credit for the Reform Act of 1832.

# Alison Square

Here in Potterrow on the first floor over the passage into General's Entry (widened and the building demolished to form Marshall Street) was the home of Miss Nimmo, where Robert Burns first met Mrs Agnes Maclehose on 4 December 1787 at a tea party. They met again on 12 January 1788 when Burns arrived by sedan chair as he had injured his leg. In the interval the two flirted and then corresponded as 'Clarinda' and 'Sylvander' in letters of extravagant passion. Here also the English poet Thomas Campbell (1777-1844) lived for a time and wrote his poem 'The Pleasures of Hope' (1799).

# The Queen's Hall

One of the most intimate and best-proportioned concert halls in Edinburgh is the Queen's Hall which stands on Nicolson Street half a mile south of Alison Square and facing the hills of the Queen's Park. Built in

1823 as the Hope Park Chapel, the Queen's Hall was opened by the Queen in 1979 and is the home of the Scottish Chamber Orchestra. Jazz is also a feature of the Hall's regular programme.

*The Queen's Hall, built as a church in 1823 and re-opened as a concert hall in 1979 in the presence of Her Majesty the Queen.*

Crossing over towards the Queen's Park we come to **'Hermits and Termits'**, No 64 St Leonard's Street, built in 1734 and restored in 1981 having been a railway office for many years. Its gate is made of floral ironwork, its harled walls are yellow, and the crest above the front door shows a blue swan over a coronet.

In front of the house is a paved area where the Waterloo well has been tastefully and safely sited some yards from its original position in Parkside Street so as to form a feature. At one time the house belonged to Robert Scott, an engraver. His two sons William (a Pre-Raphaelite painter) and David (1806-49) a painter of imaginative scenes from history, were brought up in the house.

At 35 **Lutton Place** Sir William Russell Flint (1880-1969) was born. He served his apprenticeship in an Edinburgh printing-works as a lithographic artist (1894-1900). In London he was a medical illustrator and then was a staff artist on *The Illustrated London News*. After war service he became a painter (mainly in water-colour), his best-known works being voluptuous studies of Spanish girls.

Behind the drab facade of No 17 **Melville Terrace** (on the top floor) was for a number of years the home of the international operatic tenor Joseph Hislop (1884-1977) who began his musical career as a chorister at St Mary's Cathedral, Palmerston Place. He served an apprenticeship as a photo-process engraver in Edinburgh, before going to Sweden where he became a leading tenor at the Royal Swedish Opera, Stockholm. Engagements in Italy (including La Scala, Milan) followed and tours of North and South America, Australia, New Zealand and South Africa. Hislop appeared on numerous occasions at Covent Garden (with Melba and the Russian bass Chaliapin) and made over 150 records before turning to a successful career as a Professor of Singing.

Only a short walk south brings us to No 7 **Braid Place**. Facing the street is the back of what used to be Sciennes Hill House (1741), the home of Professor Adam Ferguson (1723-1816), an ex-military chaplain, and Professor of Natural and Moral Philosophy at Edinburgh. A plaque can be seen (from what is now the back-green of the house – originally the front) recording the fact that sometime during the winter of 1786-87 the 16-year-old Walter Scott was the only person (in the distinguished company) who could identify the lines of poetry written under a print of a dead soldier which Burns admired. Burns gave the young Scott a glance of admiration and added 'You'll be a man yet sir!' Scott only saw Burns once more – while the latter was examining a bookstall in Parliament Square. On that occasion Burns did not notice him.

# FIRST NEW TOWN
# Calton Hill

## Nelson Monument

Before attempting to climb the 143 steps to the top of the Monument it should be pointed out that this may be an undue strain for persons with heart or other conditions. The base of the Monument is 456 feet above sea-level and its height is 106 feet (this compares with the 440 feet above sea-level of Edinburgh Castle and the 200 feet of the Scott Monument). Built on the Calton Hill south-east of the Observatory the Monument was designed in 1807 by William Burn. It is over 30 metres in height with six stages corresponding to an inverted telescope. From its roof the finest panoramic view of Edinburgh can be had. A certificate can be bought for those who manage to get to the top. Above the entrance is a carving of the stern of a Spanish ship (the San Josef), which with its three decks and 112 guns was the flagship of Admiral Don Josef de Cordova at the Battle of Cape St Vincent in 1797. Nelson captured the warship and the Admiral was killed. Inside the entrance three relief carvings of a warship with 56 guns on each side are on the wall and the legend 'England expects that every man this day will do his duty.' A model of the *Victory* stands in a glass case, there is a plaster bust of Admiral Lord Nelson and an engraving of the British Lion tearing the French flag.

Originally there was to have been accommodation for veterans in the building but now it functions as a tourist attraction and as a guide to shipping in the Forth. The time-ball drops at 12 noon GMT (1 pm in summer) on weekdays. In summer the drop coincides with the firing of the 1 o'clock gun from Edinburgh Castle. On 1 October every year (the anniversary of the Battle of Trafalgar) naval flags fly from the Monument proclaiming Nelson's famous signal: 'England expects that every man this day will do his duty'.

# The Observatory

The **Old Observatory** (now known as Rock House) was designed by James Craig (the architect of the New Town) and, at the suggestion of Robert Adam, made to look like a fortified tower. Completed in 1792 it later became the home and studio of the pioneer photographer David Octavius Hill. The **New Observatory** (begun in 1818 and designed by William Playfair) is in the shape of a cross of four Doric temples with a high central dome and a boundary wall at whose south-eastern corner is a monument to Playfair's uncle, Professor John Playfair (1748-1819), President of the Astronomical Association. When George IV visited Edinburgh in 1822 he gave permission for the title of Royal Observatory to be used.

The most brilliant of Edinburgh's Professors of Astronomy was Charles Piazzi Smyth (1819-1900). After he had visited the Imperial Observatory near St Petersburg, Russia, Piazzi Smyth sent back his stereographs to his friends in Russia but they were lost with the ship carrying them, the *Edinburgh*, which sank some time after leaving Leith.

In 1864, preoccupied with mystical speculation, he set off to Egypt to explore the Great Pyramid at Giza near Cairo, convinced that the early Egyptians knew the value of the mathematical equation 'Pi' and that the Pyramid had been built as a standard of terrestrial

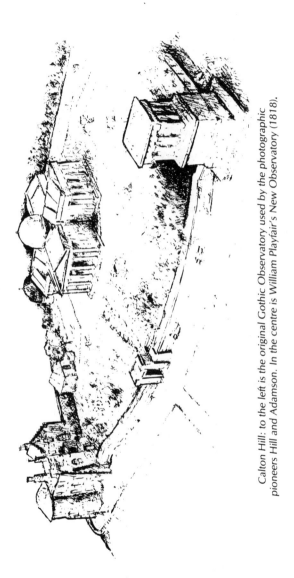

Calton Hill: to the left is the original Gothic Observatory used by the photographic pioneers Hill and Adamson. In the centre is William Playfair's New Observatory (1818).

weights and measures. To help his researches he became a pioneer in the use of miniature cameras and was one of the first to use a flash (made of a mixture of magnesium and gunpowder). While in Egypt Piazzi Smyth took 160 photographs of both the exterior and the interior of the Great Pyramid.

To the west is the delicate circular temple in memory of Dugald Stewart (1753-1828), Professor of Moral Philosophy. Lord Cockburn remembers of his old teacher that 'To me Stewart's lectures were like the opening of the heavens. I felt I had a soul. His noble views, unfolded in glorious sentences, elevated me into a higher world.'

# National Monument

Of all Edinburgh's classical temples the National Monument is the most awe-inspiring, a half-finished dream, the fragment of a vision: Scotland's tribute to the fallen of the Napoleonic Wars and to great Scots. If completed, the National Monument (designed in part by Playfair also) would have given Edinburgh a copy of the Parthenon of Athens and a mirror-image almost of the Acropolis, defining even more clearly Edinburgh's importance as an international intellectual capital. As it was, the money to be raised by subscription did not materialise and all that remains are the giant pillars of Craigleith stone, each of such weight that twelve horses and 70 men were needed to bring them up the hill. Having begun in 1823, construction stopped in 1829 with only twelve columns erected at the west end of the Monument.

*The National Monument.*

# Regent Road

To the south of the Calton Hill is the second site of the **Royal High School**, designed by Thomas Hamilton. In 1829 the High School moved from its old premises in Infirmary Street to the foot of the Calton Hill. Seven hundred pupils made up the procession from the Old Town, preceded by the band of the 17th Lancers, each class marching with a master at its head, followed by the High Constables, the magistrates, professors of the University and all those gentlemen who had attended the High School.

Among the pupils of the High School at this period were the exiled French Princes and HRH the Prince of Wales (later Edward VII) who in 1859 studied Roman history under the Rector. The Royal High School is also able to make the unusual boast of having educated an Anglican Archbishop of Canterbury and a Roman Catholic Archbishop.

Across the road from the High School (now an empty but beautiful shell, the school itself having removed to Barnton) is **St Andrew's House** (1939), the seat of Government in Scotland (the Scottish Office). Behind can be seen part of the fortified retaining-wall and the Governor's House of the former **Calton Jail** (1817), once Scotland's largest prison. One debtor described his cell as 'a small, square room, 12 feet by 9 feet, the walls and roof of which were white as snow. The floor was stone. An iron bed, one chair, and a small table comprised the furniture.'

In 1878 a French teacher, Eugene Chantrelle, was hanged in the Calton Jail for poisoning his wife after having had an affair with one of his 16-year-old pupils at the Newington Academy. The directors of the City of Glasgow Bank were imprisoned for fraud in 1879 for embezzling five million pounds while a group of Irish patriots, charged with conspiring to blow up the gasometer at Possil Park, Glasgow, were at first held in the Jail. Among political activists imprisoned in the Calton Jail were John Maclean who spent a month there in 1916, deprived of books, writing materials, cigarettes and his own clothes. Later he was joined by James Maxton. In 1919 the late Manny Shinwell took part in a demonstration in Glasgow's George Square and was sentenced at the Court of Session in Edinburgh to five months in the Jail.

A hundred yards east down Regent Road is the classical **Burns Monument** by Thomas Hamilton (1830). Originally the Monument contained Flaxman's statue of the poet (now in the Scottish National Portrait Gallery) and relics of Burns (now in Lady Stair's House).

Past the Regent Bridge into the east end of Princes Street we come to Robert Adam's **Register House** (1774-1822) which was built to house the national records of Scotland. Behind it is New Register House (1863) which maintains the registration records of births, marriages and deaths (registration having become compulsory in 1855). This also houses the office of the Lord Lyon, which keeps the Scottish genealogical records. Other records are held in **West Register House** (Charlotte Square, off the west end of Princes Street).

The earliest surviving Scottish public record is a letter of 1189 sent by Richard I ('Coeur de Lion') to restore Scottish independence. Records were at first kept in Edinburgh Castle but after being transported to England on at least two occasions (1296 and 1650) they were placed in the Laigh (Low) Parliament House so as to be close to the Court of Session. In 1789 they were deposited in General Register House.

Searching for information on Scottish ancestors is best begun at the General Register Office for Scotland at New Register House. Here the old parish registers and birth, marriage and death certificates post-1855 are kept, as well as census returns and monumental inscriptions. The services of the Lord Lyon, King of Arms, can be called upon for information on coats of arms and recorded genealogies. It should now be possible to set about drawing up a family tree. Other different sources of information can be had at the Scottish Record Office in Old Register House. These include Wills, the Register of Sasines (heritable property from 1617), and records which list individuals: Diligence records (legal processes for the enforcement of obligations), Court of Session records (useful in the case of bankruptcies), Court of Justiciary records (criminal), Taxation schedules, Valuation Rolls and Church, Burgh or Estate records. Specific enquiries about Edinburgh can also be answered by the Archivist of the City of Edinburgh District Council at the **City Chambers**.

Behind Register House are the remains of a once fashionable quarter, St James Square (the carved stone name has been set up as a monument). Here, at the home of William Cruikshank (one of the teachers at the High School), Robert Burns came to stay in 1787. Here Burns found himself confined to his room with a bruised leg (which a drunken coachman had given him) and suffering from concussion. His accident led to the passionate correspondence with Mrs Maclehose ('Clarinda' to his 'Sylvander'). Burns' room was in the attic of the gable facing the Post Office.

# The Scott Monument

The Scott Monument in Princes Street is a memorial to one of Scotland's most influential personalities who, through his novels, verse, and his genius for public relations, made Scotland into a universal symbol for thrilling adventures and romantic pageantry (not always fashionable today) which caught the imagination of the world.

Sir Walter Scott, like Henry Lord Cockburn, involved himself in the life of Scotland at many different levels. It is interesting to remember that, like Robert Louis Stevenson, Scott was a lawyer, an advocate, – for in many ways Scottish culture was preserved by the multifarious activities of the legal profession (including men like Francis Jeffrey, founder and editor of the influential *Edinburgh Review*). Scott became a symbol of Scotland and the Scott Monument, whose foundation-stone was laid in 1840, commemorates his achievement in revitalising the sense of identity of the Scottish nation.

When George IV visited Edinburgh in 1822 the event was carefully stage-managed by Scott, who arranged for the 're-discovery' of the Scottish Regalia in Edinburgh Castle, the tartan-swathed reception at Holyrood, and the dedication ceremonies on the Calton Hill (intended as Scotland's national shrine). It was Scott's powerful novels and his collections of the vigorous ballads of his own Scottish Borders which restored confidence and identity to a country which had lost its Crown and its Parliament, and suffered ruthless subjugation after the Jacobite Rebellions. The Carrara marble statue of Scott by the tireless Sir John Steell (1804-91) shows him sitting with his deer-hound Maida at his feet as if gazing out from the slope of a Border hill, a book propped on his knee and a pencil in his hand. The lower part of the Monument is decorated with the images of 16 Scots poets and three monarchs; the 64 niches of the Monument each contain a statuette of a character from one of Scott's novels or a famous figure in Scottish history.

*The Scott Monument.*

# Princes Street

The south-facing fronts of Princes Street have so completely changed that little trace of the originals remains. In the first block between **West Register Street** and **South St Andrew Street** were once the premises of the most influential publishers in Britain: at No 10 Archibald Constable and at No 17 William Blackwood.

The shop of Archibald Constable (1774-1827) to which he came in 1822, was the scene of a new dimension in publishing. Constable had begun as a lad in the bookshop of Peter Hill in Parliament Close. Hill had acted for Robert Burns in commercial matters for he was City Treasurer and a Governor of

Heriot's Hospital. Constable in 1795 set up on his own as a bookseller and publisher on the north side of the High Street. In 1801 he took over the *Scots Magazine* and in 1802 published the first number of the *Edinburgh Review*. In 1812 he bought over the copyright and stock of the *Encyclopaedia Britannica*. Constable, whose business style was characterised by inflated prices and extraordinary generosity, began an association with Sir Walter Scott, publishing his novels. However, in 1827 financial disaster struck which was to wear down even Constable's optimism and giant frame; he died in that year, dragging Scott into financial ruin.

At No 17 Princes Street *Blackwood's Magazine* was born under its editor, the publisher William Blackwood. Blackwood was born in Edinburgh in humble circumstances and apprenticed at Bell & Bradfute in Parliament Close. Having spent some time in Glasgow and London he returned to Edinburgh and set up in business on the South Bridge as a dealer in antiquarian books. In 1810 he helped to found the *Edinburgh Britannica*. In 1816 he moved to Princes Street, to premises frequented by Tory literary men. As in his future establishment at No 45 George Street, his Princes Street business was laid out in an enticing series of compartments drawing the visitor into the heart of the building – 'an elegant oval saloon, lighted from the roof, where various groups of loungers and literary dilettanti are engaged in looking at, or criticising amongst themselves, the publications just arrived by that day's coach from town,' (as J G Lockhart noted). Archibald Constable and William Blackwood are buried close together in a secluded corner of the Old Calton Burial Ground not far from their business premises.

At No 6 **North St David Street** lived Sir Walter Scott from March to July 1826, lodging with a Mrs Brown after the death of his wife and the breaking up of his home in North Castle Street. Scott was in mourning but had his butler from Abbotsford in attendance.

For the last part of his life the home of the philosopher and historian David Hume (1711-76) was at No 21 **South St David Street**. James Nasmyth (the inventor of the steam-hammer) in his autobiography writes that 'My grandfather built the first house in the south-west corner of St Andrew Square, for the occupation of David Hume the historian, as well as the two most important houses in the centre of the north side of the same square.' On the wall of this house occurred the humorous incident which gave the street its curious name. Wanting to poke fun at the agnostic Hume who, although a kind and generous friend, strongly disbelieved in the existence of God, some of his acquaintances wrote 'SAINT DAVID STREET' on his wall. Seeing it in the morning, Hume's young maid ran to tell her master, expecting an explosion of indignation. Instead, Hume saw the funny side of the *graffiti* and all ended happily with the facetious title being laughingly adopted by the people of Edinburgh.

## St Andrew Square

Returning to the north-west corner of St Andrew Square (No 21) we find the house in which Henry Lord Brougham (1778-1868) was born. Brougham was educated at the High School and became an advocate in 1800, being admitted to the English Bar eight years later. He became an MP in 1810, and later Lord Chancellor (1830-34). Brougham was one of the founders of the *Edinburgh Review* and popularised the carriage called after him – the 'brougham'. He also helped to found the Academy of Physics at Edinburgh (1797). In 1859 Brougham Place was named after him.

On the east side of the Square (Nos 34-35) is a building once known as the Douglas Hotel. Here in 1832 Sir Walter Scott spent his last two nights in Edinburgh.

Immediately next door is the headquarters of the Royal Bank of Scotland, designed by Sir William Chambers (1771) for Sir Laurence Dundas. In 1794 it became the Excise Office and in 1825 it was acquired by the Royal Bank. In front of the house stands the Hopetoun Monument (1834) by Thomas Campbell, which commemorates John, 4th Earl of Hopetoun (1765-1823). A professional soldier, he served in the West Indies and at Corunna commanded the left flank of the British Army. He was an MP, Captain of the Royal Archers and Governor of the Royal Bank of Scotland.

# York Place

North of St Andrew Square is **York Place** where, at No 32, Sir Henry Raeburn (1756-1823) built himself a house in 1795; the top floor was lit by skylights to provide space for exhibiting his portraits, while the lower floors were fitted out as studios for painting.

Since 1884 No 36 has been the Scottish headquarters of the Pharmaceutical Society. On display are decorated carboys, medicine bottles, ointment jars, travelling medicine chests and pill machines.

At No 47 lived the family of Alexander Nasmyth (1756-1840) the painter and engineer. He had trained as an artist with Allan Ramsay and later went to Italy where he specialised in landscapes. His most famous portrait (and probably the most authentic of all) was that of Robert Burns which he worked on in the poet's lodgings in the Lawnmarket. Nasmyth collaborated with Patrick Miller of Dalswinton in designing and testing a steamboat. One of his sons was Patrick Nasmyth (1787-1831), a landscape painter also, and another son, James Nasmyth (1808-90), was the celebrated engineer, inventor of the steam-hammer and many other innovations. The impressive Nasmyth family tomb is in the Dean Cemetery.

# Queen Street

## The Scottish National Portrait Gallery

The Scottish National Portrait Gallery in Queen Street was finished in 1890, made possible by a gift of £50 000 from the owner of *The Scotsman* newspaper, J R Findlay, with the aim of providing a visual record of men and women whose lives had been of outstanding significance. In this sense it achieved what the uncompleted National Monument on Edinburgh's Calton Hill had failed to deliver: a pantheon of the 'great and the good' in purposeful and glittering procession.

Since portrait-painting was very much a Renaissance preoccupation, the earliest periods of Scottish history before the end of the 16th century are not represented in the Gallery's collection. The invention of photography in the 19th century, a cheap, rapid and accurate rival to the painted likeness, helps to explain the relative sparseness of the Portrait Gallery's paintings after 1900 and the establishment in 1984 of the **Scottish Photography Archive** at the Portrait Gallery.

# Royal College of Physicians

Charles II granted the College's first Royal Charter in 1681. The intention of the 21 original Fellows was not only to advance the practice of medicine but to improve prevention of disease and the relief of suffering (especially among the poor). Originally housed in Fountain Close off the High Street, the College built a new hall in George Street (designed by James Craig) and moved there in 1781. However, the building was sold in 1834 and soon afterwards demolished. Today the College has substantial premises at No 9 **Queen Street** (a building completed in 1846).

To the west down Queen Street is No 52 which was the home of Sir James Young Simpson (1811-70) from 1845 to the year of his death. Chambers *Biographical Dictionary* records that 'In his house and at his table there were always to be found men and women of all countries, classes, opinions, and pursuits'. The discovery of the anaesthetic properties of chloroform was made here in 1847 as Simpson himself describes:

'I had the chloroform beside me for several days, but it seemed so unlikely a liquid to produce results of any kind, that it was laid aside; and on searching for another object among some loose papers, after coming home very late one night, my hand chanced to fall upon it; and I poured some of the fluid into tumblers before my assistants, Dr George Keith and Dr Duncan, and myself. Before sitting down to supper we all inhaled the fluid, and were all under the mahogany in a trice, to my wife's consternation and alarm.'

Next door at No 53 Professor John Wilson (1785-1854) lived before moving to Ann Street in 1819 and to Gloucester Place in 1825. Here 'Christopher North' (Wilson's pen-name in *Blackwood's Magazine*) dreamed up the 'Chaldee Manuscript', a Biblical story supposed to be the translation of a recently-unearthed manuscript but in fact a thinly-disguised satire on Edinburgh personalities. It was published in the October 1817 edition of *Blackwood's Magazine*.

Francis Lord Jeffrey (1773-1850) was living at No 62 at the time when *The Edinburgh Review* was first printed (1802). His apartments were third-rate but Jeffrey, after a morning at the Courts in Parliament House, spent his afternoons receiving clients, and as Archibald Constable noted, would 'write law pleadings, dine out, attend his evening parties, flutter with the lively and the gay, pay homage to beauty, till the night was far spent, and then return home to write an article for the *Review*, until the morning light found him still awake and working in his study.'

# The Hopetoun Rooms

Designed by Thomas Hamilton (1827), the Hopetoun Rooms were once Edinburgh's finest concert-hall. In January 1841 the Hungarian virtuoso pianist Franz Liszt gave a recital in the Rooms and delighted his audience by playing on themes as they were jotted down for him by members of the audience. Seven years later (in October 1848) the Polish composer and pianist Fryderyk Chopin gave a two-hour evening concert in the Hopetoun Rooms. The *Scotsman* wrote that 'the infinite delicacy and finish of his playing, combined with great occasional energy never overdone, is very striking when we contemplate the man – a slender and delicate-looking person, with a marked profile, indicating much intellectual energy.'

The *Edinburgh Advertiser* wrote: 'while all other pianists strive to equalise the power of the fingers, M. Chopin aims to utilise them and, in accordance with this idea, are his treatment of the scale and the shake, as well as his mode of sliding with one and the same finger, from note to note, and of passing the third over the fourth finger.' Most of 'the elite of Edinburgh society were present' and the critic notes that 'we have rarely seen such a display of rank and beauty congregated at a similar entertainment.' Chopin did not neglect his fellow-countrymen in the audience: he played two Polish melodies 'somewhat peculiar in style, yet very pleasing. That they went home to the hearts of such of the performer's compatriots as were present, was evident from the delight with which they hailed each forgotten melody.'

In 1870 the Merchant Maiden Hospital (Mary Erskine's School) took over the building. Among the many well-known former pupils is the actress Adrienne Corri (born 1932), star of film and stage. In 1964 the classical front of 1913 was replaced to form **Erskine House**.

On the north side of **Albyn Place** (No 9), a continuation of Queen Street, is the birthplace of Alan Campbell Swinton (1863-1930), a distant relation of Sir Walter Scott. Swinton's scientific achievement is illustrated at the Chambers Street Museum (Room 1.21) where a photograph of an X-ray laboratory shows how Swinton located a bullet in a man's skull using X-rays. His greatest innovation, however, was to suggest the idea of electronic television through cathode ray tubes. It was this method which was adopted by the BBC, not that of John Logie Baird who in 1926 first sent moving pictures through space.

# Charlotte Square

Now we climb south up to **North Charlotte Street** to No 45 Charlotte Square (on the north-east side of the

Square). From 1898 to 1938 this was the home of Sir Robert Philip (1857-1939), who was largely responsible for the conquest of the killer disease, tuberculosis. Philip studied medicine at Edinburgh and, after further research, in 1887 opened the Victoria Dispensary for Consumption in Bank Street (off the Lawnmarket) developing what became known as 'The Edinburgh System' of visiting homes where cases of tuberculosis had been found. By 1894 the clinic had become the Royal Victoria Hospital for Consumption. Sir Robert Philip was knighted in 1913, became President of the Royal College of Physicians and Professor of Tuberculosis at Edinburgh in 1917.

Turning west the visitor comes to No 5 (now the offices of the National Trust for Scotland) which was the birthplace of Sir Leander Starr Jameson (1853-1917), whose father was a Writer to the Signet. Jameson studied medicine in London before going to South Africa in 1878 as a partner in a medical practice in Kimberley (the gold-town) where he met the young Cecil Rhodes. Dr Jameson resigned his medical practice in 1889 to set off with a trader to deliver rifles and ammunition to Lobengula, King of the Matabele (whom he cured from gout).

In the famous 'Jameson Raid' (1895) he made an unsuccessful attempt to come to the assistance of the Outlanders (who were in dispute with the Boer Government) at the head of 600 men. Jameson was ambushed by the Boers at Krugersdorp and he and his remaining 250 men were surrounded by 3000 Boers. After Jameson's surrender he was sentenced to be shot but fortunately President Kruger refused to sign the order. The 'Jameson Raid' was, however, the spark that eventually led to the Boer War (1899-1902) after which Jameson became Progressive Premier of the Cape Colony and was made a baronet in 1911.

In the middle of the south-facing block (No 6) is the official residence of the Secretary of State for Scotland, **Bute House**, at one time owned by Sir John Sinclair (1754-1835) organiser of the Statistical Account of Scotland; his daughter, Catherine Sinclair, the author, is commemorated in the Gothic monument at the junction of St Colme and North Charlotte Streets.

# The Georgian House

The 'Georgian House' at No 7 on the north side of Charlotte Square is part of the elegant yet simple facade created by the architect Robert Adam at the suggestion, in 1790, of the Lord Provost. Charlotte Square was the final section of the First New Town: the feus of the north side were put on sale in 1792, a matter of days after Adam's death. No 7 was built in 1796 and sold to John Lamont. In 1975 it was opened to the public as a restored National Trust property.

At No 9 lived Lord Joseph Lister, a pioneer in the use of antiseptics.

Crossing over to the west side of the Square we arrive at No 14 where Henry, Lord Cockburn (1779-1854) lived from 1812 to 1830, one of the key figures in the cultural history of Edinburgh (after whom the Cockburn Association is named), a writer of absorbing memoirs with a genius for the description of character.

'Cockburn', writes Dr Guthrie, 'was a man of fascinating manners and fine genius; the greatest orator, in one sense, I ever heard.' Thomas Carlyle gives this picture: 'a bright, cheery-voiced, large-eyed man, a Scotch dialect with plenty of good logic in it.' The *Edinburgh Review* in 1857 adds that he was 'rather below the middle height, firm, wiry and muscular, inured to active exercise of all kinds, a good swimmer, an accomplished skater, and an intense lover of the fresh breezes of heaven.' Cockburn was Solicitor-General in 1830 and seven years later a Lord of Justiciary. As one of the leaders of the Scottish Whigs he helped to draft the First Reform Bill for Scotland. The rest of his days he spent in his country seat at Bonaly.

In the centre of the west side of the Square is **West Register House**, designed as a church by Robert Reid, dating from 1814, its dome being modelled on that of St Paul's Cathedral. Today it houses maps, plans, most modern Government records, railway records, those of the nationalised industries, legal records post-1800 and the private archives of industry and commerce. It also contains the **Scottish Record Office Museum**.

Among the documents on display to the public are

the Treaty of Edinburgh of 1328 negotiated by Robert I and Edward III of England; an inventory of the embroideries of Mary Queen of Scots; charges of witchcraft against Janet Boyman of the Cowgate who was convicted and burnt in 1572; a letter from Oliver Cromwell to Lieutenant-General David Leslie, commander of the Covenanter army, concerning the exchange of prisoners; the Articles of Union between England and Scotland (1706). Among the letters on view are those of Robert Adam, James Boswell, David Hume, Sir Henry Raeburn, Adam Smith, Robert Louis Stevenson, Thomas Telford, James Watt and Robert Burns.

At the west corner of the southern block, at No 24, Field Marshal Lord Haig was born (*see*: Huntly House Museum 2nd Floor – Rooms 16, 17, 18). At No 16 South Charlotte Street Alexander Graham Bell (1847-1922) was born. He was a pupil at the High School (1858-62) and then moved to London. Alexander's father was a Professor of elocution and challenged his son to make a speaking machine. This he and his brother did, building it out of a lambs' larynx, rubber sheeting and a gutta-percha moulding of the human skull and jawbone. To this were added rubber lips, a wooden tongue and a soft palate stuffed with cotton-wool. Blowing into a metal tube the brothers were able to make the head say 'Mama' so convincingly that the neighbours at No 13 were heard to ask: 'What can be the matter with the baby?'

# George Street

From South Charlotte Street the visitor turns right into George Street; in 1798, soon after his marriage, Sir Walter Scott left his parents' house in George Square to lodge for a short time here at No 108 while waiting for his new house at No 39 North Castle Street to be readied.

Kenneth Grahame (1859-1932), the author of *The Wind in the Willows*, was born at No 32 Castle Street, the son of an advocate. When he was only five his mother died and the family moved south.

To No 10 **Castle Street** came Shelley with his wife

and small child in 1813, on the run from his creditors. In August Shelley came of age and he married Harriet again in an Episcopal church in Edinburgh.

Sir Walter Scott moved into his new home at No 39 **North Castle Street** in 1798 and was to stay there for 28 years. 'Scott's house in Edinburgh is divinely situated,' the poet Samuel Taylor Coleridge noted, 'it looks up a street full upon the rock and castle.'

In this house, in his study behind the dining-room, Scott finished *Waverley* (1814) and *Guy Mannering* (1815) and in one year (1823) completed *Peveril of the Peak*, *Quentin Durward* and *St Ronan's Well*. Scott worked as Writer to the Signet in Parliament House every morning and then spent the rest of the day writing. In his study Scott wrote at a massive table with the help of a fine old box richly carved and lined with red velvet. Only one picture hung in the sombre room, one of John Graham of Claverhouse, 'Bonnie Dundee' (1648-89). It hung over the fireplace, a Highland targe (shield) on either side, broadswords and dirks radiating from them.

Returning to George Street we find No 92 to which Francis Jeffrey came in 1810 from Queen Street (see above). Here Jeffrey lived for over 18 years and Thomas Carlyle describes his study in 1827: 'a roomy, not over neat apartment on the ground floor, with a big baize-covered table loaded with book-rows and paper bundles. Five pairs of candles were cheerfully burning, in the light of which sat my famous little gentleman.'

At No 60 was the house where the English poet Percy Bysshe Shelley (1792-1822) stayed in early September 1811 with his newly-married wife Harriet (he was 19 and she 16), having eloped from London. Thomas Jefferson Hogg writes: 'I soon set foot in George Street, a spacious, noble, well-built street; but a deserted street, or rather a street which people had not yet come fully to inhabit. I soon found the number indicated at the post-office. I have forgotten it, but it was on the left side – the side next to Princes Street. I knocked at the door of a handsome house; it was all right; and in a handsome front-parlour I was received rapturously by my friend.'

'It was the year of the famous comet,' continues Hogg, 'and of the still more famous vintage, the year 1811; the weather was fine, and often hot; not one drop of rain fell all the time I was in Edinburgh. The nights were clear and bright; we often contemplated the stranger comet from Princes Street.'

Perhaps the most popular building in the New Town was the **Assembly Rooms** and the **Music Hall** (both situated at No 54 George Street).

# The Assembly Rooms and Music Hall

The Assembly Rooms (not to be confused with the Church of Scotland's Assembly Hall on the Mound) were designed by John Henderson and first opened on Thursday 11 January 1787 with the Ball of the Caledonian Hunt. The new Assembly Rooms were the largest in Britain (except for those in Bath), being 92 feet long, 42 feet broad and 30 feet high. The first Assembly Rooms in Edinburgh were in the West Bow and later three others in the High Street (Old and New Assembly Closes) and Buccleuch Place. Two of the older venues were by 1787 a guardhouse and a stationery warehouse.

The novelist, Oliver Goldsmith, who while a medical student at Edinburgh (1752-54) lived near John Knox's house in the High Street, described the dancing assemblies in Old Assembly Close: 'When the stranger enters the dancing room he sees one end of the room taken up by ladies, who sit dismally in a group by themselves, and at the other end stand their pensive partners that are to be. The ladies may ogle and the gentlemen may sigh, but an embargo is laid upon any close converse. At length they perform with a formality approaching to despondency. After five or six couples have thus walked the gauntlet, all stand for the country dance, each gentleman furnished with a partner from the aforesaid lady directress. So they dance and say nothing, and this concluded an assembly.'

Twenty years later the Englishman Captain Topham described an assembly in New Assembly Close: 'As the room is too small for the company, the Lady

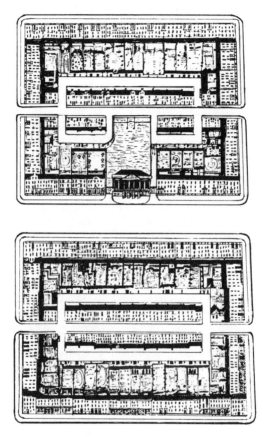

*The New Town: Rose Street and Thistle Street with the Assembly Rooms. James Craig's grid-iron plan of 1766 with its rectangular symmetry.*

Directress is obliged to divide the company into Sets, and suit them according to their rank and quality, putting about twelve couples in a Set.'

The 60-strong membership of the Caledonian Hunt who opened the Assembly Rooms in George Street consisted of 17 noblemen, 11 baronets and others (mostly gentlemen with very large estates). Each member was allocated two ladies' tickets and one gentleman's: in all about 340 people attended. At the time of the opening of the Assembly Rooms the poet Robert Burns was in Edinburgh to oversee the printing of a new edition of his poems. The Caledonian Hunt had agreed to subscribe for 100 copies and allowed Burns to dedicate the volume to the Hunt. Burns, however, does not seem to have been invited to the Ball at the Assembly Rooms.

In October 1843 the Music Hall (designed by David Bryce and William Burn) was built behind the Assembly Rooms. The new Hall was in the shape of a cross with arms of equal length. To the south was the stage, to the north a U-shaped gallery. The Music Hall was used for many public events, both artistic and political. Here the Freedom of Edinburgh was granted to Benjamin Disraeli (1867), and in November 1879 William Ewart Gladstone launched his Midlothian campaign. In 1866 Thomas Carlyle was installed as Rector of Edinburgh University (the McEwan Hall had not yet been built). In both World Wars the Music Hall was used as a recruiting centre.

# The Royal Society of Edinburgh

In 1783 the first Charter of the Royal Society of Edinburgh was granted by George III. The first formal meeting was held in the College (University) Library under the chairmanship of the Principal, William Robertson. The aim of the Society was to serve both science and literature equally, and it was intended that the new body should be a National Academy for Scotland. There were two classes in the Society – the Physical and the Literary. However, Sir Walter Scott was its only literary President (1820-32) while Robert Louis Stevenson's papers (1872-73) were the only contributions by a major literary figure. The Literary class was soon eclipsed by the Physical and in time disappeared.

## The Edinburgh Merchant Company

The administration of the public affairs of the Burgh of Edinburgh was in the hands of the Town Council from medieval times to 1832. The Council was composed of merchants and members of craft guilds (some 14 of these existed by 1600). These were the two exclusive commercial classes: below them in the social scale came journeymen, servants, labourers, beggars, vagabonds and gypsies.

While the craft guilds were licensed to manufacture the finer articles, they did not have permission to indulge in trade outside the Burgh. This was the prerogative of the merchants (many of whom began as craft apprentices and when they owned a business, set themselves up as merchants). The Charter of Incorporation of the Company of Merchants of the City of Edinburgh dates from 1681 when Charles II signed a Warrant to that effect. The first meeting of the Merchant Company took place in the High Council House. In 1691 the Merchant Company moved into their own permanent premises in the Cowgate (then one of the most fashionable areas) in what is now Merchant Street (off Candlemaker Row and under George IV Bridge). Almost one hundred years later the Company took possession of a purpose-built Company Hall behind the Tron in Hunter Square, whose elegant facade by John Baxter can be seen to this day. The Merchant Company moved finally to its present Merchants Hall in Hanover Street in 1879.

## National Gallery of Scotland

The National Gallery was designed and built by William Henry Playfair (1790-1857) in 1854 in warm pink stone and with the curly capitals of the smooth Ionic style. The Gallery stands at the foot of the Mound behind the Royal Scottish Academy (built by Playfair in the colder pastel yellows of Craigleith stone in 1826 and enlarged in 1836 in the severely fluted Doric order. The origins of the National Collection lie in purchases made by The Royal Institution (founded 1819) and The Royal Scottish Academy (founded 1826). To these were added loans and gifts.

# NORTHERN NEW TOWN

The portrait painter Sir Henry Raeburn (1756-1823) was born into a working-class family in Stockbridge. He was at first apprenticed to a goldsmith and then to David Deuchar, a seal-engraver. By chance David Martin, Scotland's leading portrait artist of his day, saw Raeburn at work, was impressed by his talent and engaged him as an apprentice. Raeburn in time became the finest painter of portraits in Scotland. In 1780 he married the widow of Count Leslie and so acquired the house and estate of Deanhaugh, later adding the estate of St Bernard's.

**Ann Street** is famous as one of the most charming of Edinburgh streets: it was named after Raeburn's wife and stands on a secluded rise above the Water of Leith, two rows of houses facing each other across their front gardens. At No 29 John Wilson (1785-1854) – otherwise known as 'Christopher North' – lived from 1819 to 1826. Wilson's daughter (and biographer) writes: 'Towards the end of the winter of 1819 my father with his wife and children, five in number, left his mother's house, 53 Queen Street, and set up his household gods in a rural and somewhat inconvenient house in Ann Street.'

Travelling down Dean Terrace to Stockbridge, we climb Gloucester Street to **Duncan's Land**, now a restaurant, but in 1796 the birthplace of David Roberts (1796-1864). Roberts' father was a shoemaker but young David showed early artistic talent (expressed in charcoal on the white-washed kitchen wall of their home) and so, at the age of twelve, he was apprenticed to a painter and decorator.

During the years of his apprenticeship Roberts learnt all the tricks of the interior decoration trade:

how to give the illusion of marble, wood or even that of a three-dimensional scene. When he qualified as a journeyman Roberts was hired by a travelling circus to maintain backcloths and paint new ones. This was invaluable training in a more voluptuous style and good preparation for his next employment – as a scene-painter for a number of British theatres (he even had, in emergencies, to appear on stage).

Returning to Edinburgh in 1818 Roberts was commissioned by Francis Jeffrey to redecorate his library at Craigcrook Castle and worked also at the Theatre Royal in Shakespeare Square (where the Post Office HQ now is). After being engaged by Covent Garden Opera House as a designer he was elected President of the Society of British Artists. In the years that followed Roberts travelled to the Continent and to Egypt, returning with magnificent paintings of landscape and scenery (which were engraved and proved to be enormously popular).

At No 6 **Gloucester Place** John Wilson lived from around 1825 to his death in 1854. Of Wilson Thomas Carlyle wrote in 1827: 'A man of the most fervid temperament, fond of all stimulating things, from tragic poetry down to whisky punch. He snuffed and smoked cigars and drank liqueurs and talked in a most indescribable style. Daylight came on before we parted; indeed it was towards three o'clock as the Professor and I walked home, smoking as we went. He is a broad, sincere man of six feet, with long dishevelled hair and two blue eyes as keen as an eagle's.'

Towards the end of his life the publisher and author, Robert Chambers (1802-71) lived at No 1 **Doune Terrace**. In his memoirs we are told that 'Visitors from all parts of the world were at all times welcome at No 1 Doune Terrace, and with these might be seen commingled some of the most notable men of the time – Lord Jeffrey, Lord Cockburn, Christopher North, Lockhart, the Ettrick Shepherd, De Quincey and many wits and conversationalists.'

Now we turn into **Moray Place** where at No 19 in the east-facing end of the block the photographic pioneer David Octavius Hill (1802-70) lived in the latter part of his life. Hill was a painter, Secretary of the

Royal Scottish Academy, and his fruitful partnership with the photographer Robert Adamson (1821-48) produced some 3000 calotypes or 'sun-pictures' of outstanding quality and historical interest.

Sir David Brewster (1781-1868), the inventor of the kaleidoscope, an outstanding innovator in the field of optics, and Principal of United College, St Andrews, had corresponded with William Fox Talbot (1800-77) who invented the calotype in 1841 (the first paper process). Brewster's colleague Dr John Adamson (who in May 1841 took the first successful portrait photograph in Scotland) handed on the process to his younger brother, Robert. Robert Adamson moved into Rock House on the Calton Hill in 1843 and opened a studio. Rock House had a sheltered and sunny garden which Adamson was able to use to produce his calotypes in ideal conditions.

In the same year, the Church of Scotland was torn apart by the 'Disruption' in which 470 ministers left to form the Free Church. It was this momentous event that D O Hill decided to preserve on a monumental canvas in which the many participants in the Disruption would be portrayed. On Brewster's advice Hill took advantage of the calotype process to capture the likenesses of his sitters rapidly and accurately.

In 1848, after Adamson's death, Hill moved into Rock House from Inverleith Row. In 1862 he re-married after his wife's death; his new bride was the sculptor Amelia Robertson Paton (sister of Joseph Noel Paton, the artist). When Hill died she modelled her husband's bust in bronze and set it up over his grave in the Dean Cemetery (where she herself was later buried).

From George Street Francis Jeffrey came to No 42 (on the western side of Moray Place) in 1817. Thomas Carlyle spent a week there in 1828 after leaving Comely Bank. Jeffrey's involvement with the *Edinburgh Review* was over by 1829. Three years later he became Lord of Session. He spent what spare time he had at his country retreat in Craigcrook Castle and died in 1850 at his Moray Place home.

From Moray Place we travel east down Darnaway Street to **Heriot Row** where Henry Mackenzie (1745-1831), the author of *The Man of Feeling* (1771) spent the latter part of his life, at No 6 Heriot Row. Lord Cockburn remembers that: 'His excellent conversation, agreeable family, good evening parties and the interest attached to united age and reputation made his house one of the pleasantest.' Visitors who came expecting to find a man wallowing in over-emotionalism were surprised to find 'a hard-headed practical man, as full of worldly wisdom as most of his fictitious characters are devoid of it; and this without in the least impairing of the affectionate softness of his heart. In person he was thin, shrivelled and yellow – kiln-dried – with something, when seen in profile, of the clever, wicked look of Voltaire.'

Robert Louis Stevenson lived from the age of six at No 17 Heriot Row with its view over Queen Street Gardens to the heights of the New Town. In those gardens he was often taken to play by his devoted nurse, 'Cummy' (Alison Cunningham), or meandered down the Water of Leith or wandered through the mysterious groves of Warriston Cemetery.

Being confined to bed for long periods Stevenson found his imagination fired by folk tales or adventure stories told in the 'land of counterpane', the wonderful make-believe world as seen in the hillocks and valleys of a child's eiderdown. It was his early life at No 17 Heriot Row that provided the inspiration for his *Child's Garden of Verses*. In his *Nuits Blanches*, Stevenson writes: 'I remember, so long ago, the sickly child that woke from his few hours' slumber with the sweat of a nightmare on his brow, to lie awake and listen and long for the first signs of life among the silent streets. Over the black belt of the garden I saw the long line of Queen Street, with here and there a lighted window. The road before our house is a great thoroughfare for early carts. You can hear the carters cracking their whips and crying hoarsely to their horses.'

James Clerk Maxwell (1831-79) was born at No 14 **India Street**, the son of a lawyer who had a keen interest in geology. His father encouraged him to make collections of insects, rocks and flowers in Galloway (where he spent his earliest days). At the Edinburgh Academy Maxwell (who had a stutter) was small for his age and with his Galloway accent he was nicknamed 'Dafty'. Maxwell, however, had laid the foundations for a more mature curiosity: at the age of 15 his first research paper was read to the Royal Society of Edinburgh and in the following year he became a student at Edinburgh University. After Edinburgh he went to Cambridge where he produced two major scientific works: he established the foundations of modern measurement of colour and opened the door to a theory of electromagnetism which predicted the existence of waves travelling at the speed of light, made up of magnetic and electrical fields. James Clerk Maxwell therefore paved the way for the development of radio, radar and television.

J M Barrie (1860-1937) was born in Kirriemuir, the son of a weaver. During his student days at Edinburgh University he lodged with a Mrs Edwards from 1879-82 in the top flat of the north-facing West House at No 3 **Great King Street**. The author of *Peter Pan* (1904), *The Admirable Crichton* (1902) and *Dear Brutus* (1917) saw a seamier side of life as a struggling student. In *Better Dead*, Barrie gives a harrowing account of conditions in student 'digs': 'I knew three undergraduates', he writes, 'who lodged together in a dreary house at the top of a dreary street; two of them used to study until two in the morning, while the third slept. When they shut up their books they woke number three, who arose, dressed and studied until breakfast time. Among the many advantages of this arrangement the chief was that, as they were dreadfully poor, one bed did for three – if lodgings were cheap and dirty, and dinners few and far between, life was still real and earnest; in many cases it did not turn out an empty dream.'

Thomas De Quincey (1785-1859) lodged at No 9 Great King Street during the years 1830-34. The prolific contributor to *Blackwood's Magazine*, *The Edinburgh Literary Gazette* and *Tait's Edinburgh Magazine* and the author of *Confessions of an English Opium Eater* (1822) was in Edinburgh and district between 1820 and his death. Between 27 November 1833 and 24 November 1836, however, he was mainly lodged in the Debtors' Sanctuary at Holyroodhouse, allowed to go safely into Edinburgh to visit his friends only on a Sunday.

One of Edinburgh's many links with Poland is

celebrated at No 84 Great King Street where the Polish violinist and composer Felix Janiewicz (1762-1848) lived. Janiewicz was born in Vilna and went to Vienna when he was 23. At that time the 29-year-old Mozart was playing quartets with Haydn in Vienna, and Janiewicz almost certainly attended some of these concerts. He was a fine violinist and it is believed that Mozart wrote his 'Andante for a Violin Concerto' for Janiewicz. After working in Italy and Paris Janiewicz arrived in London in 1792 and made his debut there as a soloist, also playing in several of Haydn's concerts.

Appearances all over the British Isles followed, then a spell as a conductor in Liverpool and Manchester after which he came to Edinburgh, where he helped to found the 1st Edinburgh Musical Festival in 1815, playing in the opening concert as leader of the Festival orchestra – a position he held until his retirement in 1829. In 1965 the acclaimed Polish violinist Henryk Szeryng unveiled a plaque at Janiewicz's former home and also laid a wreath at his newly-discovered grave in Warriston Cemetery.

Robert Garioch Sutherland (1909-81), poet and teacher, lived at No 4 **Nelson Street**. Born in Edinburgh, he graduated from Edinburgh University and began a long career as a teacher, first in London, then in Edinburgh. On his retirement he worked for The School of Scottish Studies, George Square, as a 'lexicographer's orraman'. Garioch wrote in Scots and often gave readings of his poems. One of these, 'Address til an Elm Tree – in Queen Street Gairdens, eftir the Simmer Gale' (1962) describes a scene close to where he lived:

> 'Ye hae survived, as tho nae twist had stirred,
> thanks to your bonnie neibor in the wast,
> yon florish-heavy Hawthorn, that the blast
> left, of the thrie main branches, just ae-third.
>
> Ye dour materialist, whaes reuch sides gird
> a muckle wecht o timmer, haudin fast
> to what ye hae, ye're here, and mean to last,
> mair like a rock extruded frae the yird.'

Sir William MacTaggart (1903-81) and his wife, the

Norwegian patriot and journalist Fanny Aavatsmark, lived at No 4 **Drummond Place**. His father was one of the founders of the engineering firm MacTaggart Scott at Loanhead; his grandfather was the landscape and marine artist William MacTaggart RSA. Although dogged by ill-health as a young man he attended Edinburgh College of Art for a time. His early painting was much influenced by French cubism which he saw on his visits to France. In the 1930s he was deeply impressed by the work of the Norwegian Expressionist Edvard Munch (1863-1944). In 1938 he moved into No 4 Drummond Place.

MacTaggart taught at the Edinburgh College of Art. In 1959 he was elected President of the Royal Scottish Academy, was knighted in 1962 and elected a Fellow of the Royal Society of Edinburgh in 1967. His later paintings were characterised by lush colour, and full of vitality.

Described by his friend Alexander Scott as 'our greatest modern Scots poet of love, liquor and disenchantment', Sydney Goodsir Smith (1915-75) was the son of the Professor of Forensic Medicine at Edinburgh. In Edinburgh he lived at No 50 Craigmillar Park and at No 25 Drummond Place. Smith was for a time the art critic of *The Scotsman*: he also painted and wrote plays (the most notable being the rumbustuous *Wallace* first performed in the Assembly Hall on the Mound during the 1960 Edinburgh Festival, with Iain Cuthbertson as the giant patriot).

Although best known for his life style as one of the poets who met in Edinburgh's New Town taverns, Smith was also capable of a tender evocation of nature – as in his 'Spring in the Botanic Gardens':

'The trees are heavy with blossom –
And yet
As licht and lichtsome
As the birds that din,
Compete,
And fill all trees,
All licht,
With lustful chatter
Dartin, fidgin –
For the ae live thing is livin.'

The eccentric aesthete Charles Kirkpatrick Sharpe (1781-1851) resided at No 28 up to the time he died. He was an amateur genealogist, a man of fashion (with an antique style of dress), a 'pasticheur' with a talent for zany but obsessive (and not a little waspish) caricatures, and a musician whose calling-card was marked simply with the musical notation of 'C#'!

Previous to living in Drummond Place, Sharpe had stayed with his mother at No 93 Princes Street. Robert Chambers recalled that 'His thin effeminate figure, his voice pitched in *alt*, his attire as he took his daily walks in Princes Street, a long blue frock coat, black trousers, rather wide below, and sweeping over white stockings and neat shoes – something like a web of white cambric round his neck and a brown wig coming down to his eyebrows – had long established him as what is called a character.'

Sir Compton Mackenzie (1883-1972), the novelist, bought Nos 31 and 32 Drummond Place and lived there till his death, entertaining in the manner of a true literary lion. His series of autobiographical books and his comic masterpiece *Whisky Galore* established him as an author of international stature. Compton Mackenzie was a founder member of the Scottish National Party.

At No 7 **London Street** lived and painted the outstanding Scottish colourist Anne Redpath (1895-1965). Born in Galashiels, the daughter of a tweed designer, she used to say 'I do with a spot of red or yellow in a harmony of grey, what my father did in his tweed.' From 1920 she settled in France and then returned to Scotland in 1934. She lived at No 7 London Street from 1952-65, delighting countless art-lovers with her luminous and fragrant still-lives and paintings of churches, and her instinctive sense of balance.

In No 15 London Street a momentous event in the history of Iceland took place in 1874: there Sveinbjörn Sveinbjörnsson (1847-1927), an Icelandic piano teacher composed the National Anthem of Iceland. Born near Reykjavik, Sveinbjörnsson studied music in Denmark and Germany before coming to Edinburgh where he stayed for some 40 years, publishing a collection of Icelandic folk-songs. Before he settled in

Copenhagen Sveinbjornsson lectured in Canada and the United States. He died in Copenhagen but was buried in Reykjavik with a full State funeral.

John Playfair (1748-1819), Professor of Natural Philosophy, lived at No 10 **Albany Street** in 1818 (a year before his death). Lord Cockburn tells us that he was 'admired by all men, and beloved by all women, of whose virtues and intellect he was always the champion: society felt itself the happier and more respectable from his presence.' Playfair spent almost every summer vacation travelling through Britain or the Continent to study geological formations.

The brother of the novelist Susan Ferrier (1782-1854) lived at No 38. She had published her first novel *Marriage* in 1818 while she lived with her father in Morningside (he died in 1829). Her other novels were *The Inheritance* (1824) and *Destiny* (1831). Sir Walter Scott recalls that she was 'simple, full of humour and exceedingly ready at repartee, and all this without the least affectation of the blue-stocking.' She had lost the best part of her sight and was forced to live in a darkened room, entertaining friends only in the evening.

# EASTERN NEW TOWN

## Picardy Place

At No 11 Picardy Place (now demolished) the doctor and novelist Sir Arthur Conan Doyle (1859-1930) was born. His father, an assistant surveyor at the Scottish Office, was a skilful caricaturist and two of his paintings are in the City Art Centre's Collection. Doyle himself studied medicine at Edinburgh University (when he lived in George Square) and was a keen sportsman (he later played cricket for the MCC). His greatest achievement was his creation of Sherlock Holmes, the masterly detective who lived at No 221b Baker Street with his assistant Dr Watson. Holmes was modelled on Dr Joseph Bell, one of Conan Doyle's lecturers, and Dr Watson on the surgeon Patrick Heron-Watson. No 11 Picardy Place was demolished some years ago.

# Robert Stevenson House

This recently restored building (Nos 1-8 **Baxter's Place**) was once the office of the Stevenson family engineering firm founded by Robert Louis Stevenson's grandfather Robert (who died in the house).

Robert Stevenson's stepfather was the designer of a reflector light adopted in 1786 by the Northern Lighthouse Board as a standard for Scotland's first four lighthouses. Stevenson became his stepfather's assistant in 1790 and built his first lighthouse at Portpatrick in 1792. By 1797 he was in complete control of the business. Stevenson and his workmen spent two seasons of construction living in cramped and dangerous conditions on the Bell Rock on the Inchcape. Soon he was appointed sole engineer to the Lighthouse Commissioners (one of whom was Sir Walter Scott).

Robert Stevenson made many notable contributions to the development of the City of Edinburgh: he extended Princes Street beyond the East End and round the base of the Calton Hill, supervising the construction of the Regent Road. He produced the plan for the Calton Jail (on the site of the present St Andrew's House), planned the drainage of what was to become Princes Street Gardens, designed the first railway line to Edinburgh and directed the building of access roads on many sides of the City. Stevenson had three sons, all of whom followed him into the civil engineering profession in the family firm, all becoming engineers to the Northern Lighthouse Board.

# WESTERN NEW TOWN

## No 25 Chester Street

William Chambers (1800-83), the publisher, had his home at No 25 Chester Street during his period of office as Lord Provost (1867-70). The *Dictionary of National Biography* states that he was 'About the middle height, dark in feature, with hair that comparatively early became grey; somewhat reserved in manner, he was not always popular with those who knew him slightly. He had no special literary faculty, but his writings exhibit strong common sense, and he knew how to make a subject interesting.

It is however not as the popular writer or successful publisher, but as the good citizen that he will be longest remembered. The name of William Chambers will always be connected with the City of Edinburgh which he beautified, and the Church of St Giles which he restored.'

Chambers was apparently given to recounting the hardships of his early days when he earned his morning bread roll by reading Smollett's *Roderick Random* to the baker and his men before dawn 'seated on a folded-up sack in the sill of the window with a book in one hand and a penny candle (stuck in a bottle) in the other.'

William Chambers died three days before St Giles High Kirk (on whose restoration he had spent almost £30 000 of his own money) was reopened. In the middle of Chambers Street his statue in bronze by John Rhind (1891) stands on a base of red sandstone decorated with bronze reliefs by Hippolyte Blanc showing Literature, Liberality and Perseverance as graceful female figures.

## No 8 Howard Place

At No 8 Howard Place Robert Louis Stevenson was born. He lived there for three years before the family moved to No 1 Inverleith Place (where he was to live for four years before changing house again to No 17 Heriot Row). A familiar scene for the young Stevenson was that recorded at Heriot Row some years later in his poem *The Lamplighter*:

'My tea is nearly ready, and the sun has left the sky;
It's time to take the window to see Leerie going by;
For every night at tea-time and before you take your seat,
With lantern and with ladder he comes posting up the street.'

# No 10 Warriston Crescent

Fryderyk Chopin, the Polish composer, gave his only concert in Edinburgh at the Hopetoun Rooms (now Erskine House at Nos 68-73 Queen Street) on Wednesday 4 October 1848. During his visit to Edinburgh Chopin stayed with fellow Pole, Dr Adam Lyszcynski (a medical graduate of the University of Edinburgh), who lived in Warriston Crescent. At this time Chopin was still suffering over his recent separation from George Sand, the novelist. The weather was generally cold and breezy in Edinburgh and Chopin's visit was a miserable one. He did however find time to compose one piece of music in Edinburgh, a song called 'The Spring' (perhaps a gesture of eternal hope).

# No 21 Comely Bank

Thomas Carlyle (1795-1881), born in Ecclefechan, Annandale, first came to Edinburgh in 1809 at the age of 14 and walked the 100 miles journey. At that time he stayed in Simon Square while a student at Edinburgh University, but when he returned in 1822-24 to write and teach his lodgings were at No 2 Spey

Street (in Pilrig), where he was tormented through the nights by a howling dog chained by its master in the garden below!

For 18 months (1826-28) after his marriage to Jane Welsh (whom he had met in Edinburgh) Carlyle stayed at No 21 Comely Bank, a two-storey terraced house with a small front garden. His wife described the house to Carlyle in one of the many fascinating letters that passed between them: 'there is a real flower-garden in front, overshadowed by a far-spreading tree, while the windows look out on the greenest fields with never a street to be seen.'

Carlyle contributed to *The Edinburgh Review*, and was later to become Rector of Edinburgh University. He was author of *Sartor Resartus* (1833) and *The French Revolution* (1837). However, his first novel found no publisher and he promptly threw it on the fire.

To No 21 Comely Bank came a host of visitors to see Carlyle and his wife: Sir David Brewster, Thomas De Quincey, Professor John Wilson. Carlyle recalled that 'Many a time on a soft mild night I smoke my pipe in our little flower garden and look upon all this and think of all absent and present friends and feel that I have good reason "to be thankful I am not in Purgatory".'

# OUTER EDINBURGH (NORTH)

# Leith

Leith has an 800-year history as a commercial port, trading with Europe and the world. The Leith character is breezy and salty, full of generosity. To be a Leither is to be fiercely proud of an identity separate from Edinburgh. However, this was ignominiously surrendered in 1920 when the Port was amalgamated with Edinburgh.

It was David I (c. 1084-1153) who in 1128 first granted land and harbour rights to the Abbey of

Holyroodhouse, rights which were confirmed by a
Charter of Robert I in 1329. South Leith was held by
the Logans of Restalrig under Holyrood while North
Leith came under the direct administration of the
Abbey. No foreign goods shipped into Leith could be
sold there: they would have to be taken up to the
Edinburgh markets. By 1567 the town of Edinburgh
had become the feu superior of South Leith (the larger
half) and, around 70 years later, over North Leith.
From 1567 to 1833 the Bailies who sat in the Leith
court to pass judgement on offenders were appointed
by Edinburgh and did not as a rule even live in Leith (in
the late 18th century the journey from Edinburgh to
Leith took one hour).

## Leith Council Chamber

Built as the Leith Sheriff Court in 1828 (with
reconstruction in 1868) the Leith Town Hall and Police
Station have proved to be a popular attraction. Inside
the splendidly decorated and panelled Chamber, with
its portraits of civic dignitaries, the outstanding feature
is the 12 × 6 feet panoramic painting by Alexander
Carse (c. 1770-1843), 'Oh Happy Day', which details
the scene when George IV landed at Leith on 15
August 1822. Sailors crowd the yard-arms of a berthed
vessel, the Royal Company of Archers stand in two
lines holding their bows vertically and the Royal
Dragoon Guards flourish their sabres. In the
foreground a young pickpocket is at work!

The adjacent Police Museum is well worth a visit.

## Trinity House

Situated at No 99 Kirkgate the institution known as
Trinity House dates from around 1380 when, a levy
began to be made on every ton of merchandise loaded
or unloaded by Scottish ships at the Port of Leith. The
income from this levy was distributed to the poor.

In 1483 Our Lady's Kirk of Leith was built not far off by the mariners and skippers of Leith and by 1566 a Hospital or Almshouse was erected on the site of the present building (this function was ratified by Mary Queen of Scots and her husband Henry Lord Darnley). Some 70 years later it was necessary to set up an inquiry into the use of the funds and to formulate regulations. Letters from Charles II dated October 1636 and from James Prymrose, Clerk to the Privy Council (and father-in-law of George Heriot) are displayed to this day.

The Hospital became an Incorporation in 1797 and in the same year the Freedom of the Incorporation was given to the newly victorious Admiral Adam Duncan after the Battle of Camperdown against the Dutch. Admiral Duncan accepted the honour with gratitude and his portrait by Sir Henry Raeburn was commissioned by Trinity House (where it still stands). On entering Trinity House the ancient Charter Chest can be seen together with the ballot-box of the Incorporation. In the Master's Room is a certificate given in November 1869 to Captain Charles Mann, commanding the SS *Danube* of Leith, who made the first passage of the Suez Canal (which had not at that time been fully completed).

# OUTER EDINBURGH (EAST)

## Duddingston Kirk

Built as part of the religious revival which Malcolm Canmore (c. 1031-93) and his Queen Margaret (1046-93) brought to Scotland, the church dates from the 12th century as the curiously carved Norman door in the west bay and the chancel arch prove. Later additions to the church include the Prestonfield Aisle, constructed in 1631.

Among ministers of the church two are of outstanding interest: Robert Monteith (active 1621-60) studied at Edinburgh University before becoming a

Professor of Philosophy at the University of Saumur in France. Monteith's father was an Edinburgh burgess who leased the salmon fishings on the River Forth. After his return from France Monteith was ordained in 1630 and admitted as Minister of Duddingston in the same year. Sir James Hamilton was the owner of nearby Prestonfield House; he financed the building of the Prestonfield Aisle in 1631 but two years later Monteith had an affair with Hamilton's wife and was forced to leave the country. Arriving in France, he passed himself off as one of the Monteiths of 'Salmonnet' (a reference to his father's lease of the Forth fishings) and in due course became a Roman Catholic and was appointed secretary to Cardinal Richelieu!

A second Minister was John Thomson (1778-1840) inducted in 1805. He was an artist of talent and painted throughout his life. Sir Walter Scott was an elder at Duddingston, as was Louis Cauvin (who taught Robert Burns to speak French). To the manse came Professor John Wilson, Sir David Brewster, Francis Jeffrey, Lord Cockburn and James Hogg ('The Ettrick Shepherd'). Among the artists who visited John Thomson were J M Turner, Sir David Wilkie and Thomson's brother-in-law, Robert Scott Lauder.

## Duddingston Loch

When the Loch from the Hangman's Crag to the Manse became a sheet of glittering ice it was time for Duddingston Curling Society to gather. From its foundation in 1795 the Magistrates 'headed a curling procession to the Loch returning in the evening in similar order.' The riotous scene has been comically recorded by Charles Doyle (1832-93) in his 'Curling Match at Duddingston' and 'The Winning Shot at Duddingston' (both in The City Art Centre's collection; *see* also the curling-stone in Huntly House).

Skating was a popular pastime also. John Wilson in his *Noctes Ambrosianae* gives a vivid account of the experience: 'I was at Duddingston Loch on the great day; twa bands o' music gave a martial character to the festivities. I then drew in my mouth, puckered my cheeks, made my een look fierce, hung my head on my left shouther, put my hat to the one side and so, arms akimbo, off I went in a figure 8, garring the crowd part like clouds and circumnavigatin' the frozen ocean in the space of about two minutes.' Perhaps the most evocative image of the skater at Duddingston is 'The Rev. Robert Walker skating at Duddingston Loch' by Raeburn (see: National Gallery of Scotland).

## Sheep Heid Inn

After play, there was the Sheep Heid Inn for 'the cup that cheers' — the tavern claims to have been founded in 1360 and numbered among its earlier customers James VI (who presented an ornate snuff-mull in the form of a ram's head), Mary Queen of Scots and Bonnie Prince Charlie. One of the features of the Inn is the traditional skittle-alley.

## Prestonfield House

The name 'Prestonfield' was originally 'Priestfield' as the property belonged to a Cistercian monastery in Cumberland as early as the 13th century. Since 1376 the lands of Prestonfield have been in secular hands. The old Prestonfield House was probably a fortified stone tower. In 1681 it was burnt down in the course of a student demonstration and the present mansion erected for its owner Sir James Dick (1643-1728), Lord Provost of Edinburgh. Designed by Sir William Bruce (who remodelled Holyroodhouse), the new Prestonfield House was built in 1689.

Sir Alexander Dick (1703-85) qualified as a doctor and became a Fellow of the Royal College of Physicians, Edinburgh, in 1727. He succeeded to the estate in 1746 and ten years later was elected President of the Royal College. He entertained many men of distinction — the American scientist Dr Benjamin Franklin (1706-90) visited Prestonfield in 1759 and commemorated his pleasurable stay:

> 'Joys of Prestonfield, adieu!
> Late found, soon lost, but still we'll view
> Th'engaging scene, — oft to these eyes
> Shall the pleasing vision rise.

Cheerful meals, balmy rest,
Beds that never bugs molest,
Neatness and sweetness all round,
These – at Prestonfield we found.'

Dr Samuel Johnson and his biographer James Boswell dined at Prestonfield in November 1773: Sir Alexander noted in his diary, 'I gave Mr Johnson rhubarb seeds and some melon' – rhubarb was a daily necessity for the pernickety Englishman who fussed about his health.

Henry Lord Cockburn, who often played in the grounds of the house when a boy, leaves us this picture: 'All between the loch and the house was a sort of Dutch garden. It had several long smooth lanes of turf, anciently called bowling-alleys, fountains, carved stone seats, dials, statues and trimmed evergreen hedges. How we used to make the statues spout!' Today Prestonfield House is a hotel with a superior reputation for good food in period surroundings. In the grounds peacocks roam at will, while golfers follow the little white ball close by in the shadow of the hills.

# Portobello

In the 12th century what is now Portobello was part of the Royal Forest of Drumsheuch; up to 1750 there was scarcely a house to be seen in the area. The name 'Portobello' was taken from the pantiled stone dwelling built, near what is now the Police Station, by George Hamilton, a sailor who was in the British fleet that captured the Spanish town of Puerto Bello in Panama in November 1739. When the Spanish War ended in 1744 Hamilton retired from active service and set himself up as a cobbler and harness-maker for passing coaches and carriages. He offered food and drink to travellers and serviced the horses. He seems also to have attracted members of the racing fraternity, for by 1753 there were races at George Hamilton's on the Freegate Whins with a silver cup or a saddle for the winner.

In 1763 William Jameson, the son of an Edinburgh builder contracted for the construction of the New

Town, bought 40 acres of the Figgate estate for the deep bed of clay with which he began to manufacture building bricks. By 1779 there were three brickworks in the area. A harbour was built some ten years later (1788) for the use of the tile and brick export trade; a burn was diverted to provide power for other industries – flax mills, potteries and a soap works.

An industry of a very different kind emerged at Portobello in 1795 when the sheltered beach was provided with its first bathing-machines, so challenging the nearby Leith Sands which till that date had been Edinburgh's only bathing-resort. The Prince of Wales (later Edward VII), a student at Edinburgh under the Rector of the High School, came down to Portobello Sands nearly every morning and afterwards drilled with the 16th Lancers then stationed at Piershill Barracks.

Two mineral springs were discovered and Portobello became a 'spa' with a basin bubbling with water red with oxide of iron and sulphate of lime and magnesia. The sands were also a favourite place for duels to be fought and for military drill. As early as 1745 the beach at Portobello had been the scene for the military review conducted by Prince Charles Edward Stuart on 28 October prior to his invasion of England. In the 19th century the soldiers at Piershill Barracks, the Midlothian Yeomanry Cavalry and the Edinburgh Light Horse often drilled there.

Sir Walter Scott was Quartermaster of the Light Horse; in the intervals between the drill he would walk his powerful black horse up and down the sands on his own and from time to time he would stick in his spurs and charge into the pounding surf with the spray flying around him. In the drill itself Scott would charge at turnips set on poles, slicing them with his sabre as he passed.

The military review held at Portobello Sands on 23 August 1822 has been admirably recorded in the painting by William Turner (*see*: Scottish National Portrait Gallery), which shows the sea full of yachts, the sand obscured by the smoke of cannon, and the general public crowded into carriages or booths and being served spirits, porter and ale. It is believed that some 50 000 people were at this Portobello Review.

# INDEX